unHACK YOURSELF

YOURSELF

*Restore Yourself to Your Original Settings
and Step Into Your Most Fulfilling Life*

HELEN LEVINE

Health and Wealth
C O A C H

UnHack Yourself: Restore Yourself to Your Original Settings and Step Into Your Most Fulfilling Life
Author: Helen Levine

Published by Health & Wealth Coach
Florida, USA

www.healthandwealthcoach.com

Contact publisher for bulk orders and permission requests.

Cover design by Tamara Tyson for 3 ferns > www.3ferns.com

Interior book design and formatting by Leesa Ellis of 3 ferns > www.3ferns.com

Some names and identifying details have been changed to protect the privacy of individuals.

Printed in the USA.

Library of Congress Control Number: 2024905831

ISBN (Hardcover): 979-8-9894682-0-1
ISBN (Paperback): 979-8-9894682-1-8
ISBN (eBook): 979-8-9894682-2-5

Dedication

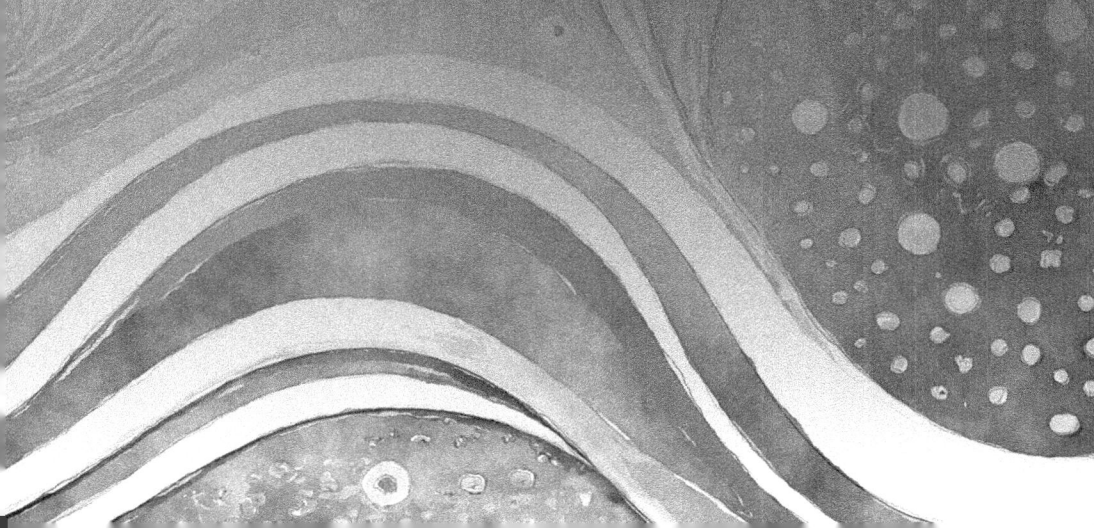

To my beloved family—the ones who saw me through every up and down; thank you for your ongoing support. My husband, Alex, you are my rock, my reflection, the wind beneath my wings. You've given me the best gift of all—self-love, which is not something I understood before I met you, and for that, I am forever grateful.

To my children, Sam and Justin, you are the why behind everything. In these pages, I want to leave you with more than just words; I want to leave you courage, lessons, and a reminder that you can always turn the page and rewrite your life story.

To my cherished clients, you've infused the essence into these pages. Guiding you in your unique journeys has been an honor and a source of inspiration, and for me, it has also been a wellspring of profound insights, understanding, and personal growth.

So, here it is—a piece of me, not just a book but a guiding light for those who follow. Each page is a snapshot of the journey I have traveled, the highs and lows, and the wisdom gained along the way. May it resonate, uplift, and inspire every reader to live richer, fuller lives.

Table of Contents

*If you don't design your own life plan,
chances are you'll fall into someone else's plan.*

Jim Rohn

Note to the Reader

What I'm about to tell you is probably not something you've ever heard before, and that is that you have been hacked. We all have been hacked. I do not mean your computer or phone has been attacked by a malicious outside force; what I'm talking about is you—your inner operating system—has been hacked from the moment you were born.

What you might not realize is that you attract people and experiences into your outward reality based on the internal programs running in the unconscious background of your inner operating system. From an early age, you have been programmed by someone's beliefs, norms, and ways to conform and behave. You were indoctrinated to certain ways of thinking, acting, and even feeling. Anything outside of that would have been considered "bad" or punishable, leaving you feeling unloved, undeserving, or unworthy. Yet underneath all those ideologies, beliefs, and programs, there is always your pure, naked, authentic consciousness available to access at any point in your life. Think of it as a return to your original factory setting.

Unhack implies that someone or something has altered your state or your system in an undesirable way, but not that you were inherently broken to begin with. It implies you've been impacted by an outside force, but not that you are damaged or defective. The idea of unhacking is about restoring yourself to your natural default state rather than fixing something that's fundamentally wrong.

All that's required for you to return to this setting is to reconnect to who you truly are— without all the stories, traumas, pains, and conditioning—and, essentially, go through a full internal system reboot. And that is what I am offering in this book.

My goal is to help you reset all the false programs that are not serving you so you can finally attract things from your true worth, not your wounds.

My goal is to help you reset all the false programs that are not serving you so you can finally attract things from your true *worth*, not your *wounds*. And that, my friend, creates a very different reality—an Unhacked You.

I never intended to be an author, but I felt compelled to share my message, personal experiences, and my journey so you do not have to suffer the way I did; you have been given a shortcut to create a better life.

I'm excited for you to take the first step on your journey to unhack your life and STEER yourself to restore yourself to your original settings and step into your most fulfilling life.

"I'm going to fly," said the caterpillar,
and everyone laughed except the butterfly.

Anonymous

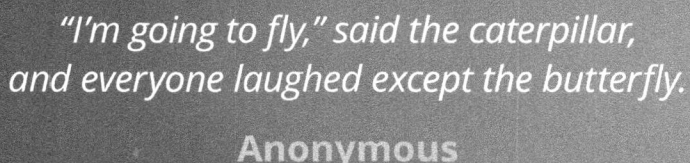

Introduction

I know what it's like to suffer, feel broken, and feel like something is wrong with you. That might sound like all doom and gloom, but at one point in my life, that's exactly how it felt for me. Just when it felt like everything was falling apart, I had a lightbulb moment when I realized that I was not broken; I was simply evolving, just like a caterpillar ready to emerge as a beautiful butterfly.

Think back to the first time you witnessed a caterpillar, humble and unassuming in its worm-like appearance, crawling along a tree branch. Not very inspiring, right? Nothing about the insect hinted at the caterpillar's true destiny at that stage of its life. It couldn't have imagined that a magical transformation would inevitably occur, and in its place, a glorious butterfly would emerge and fly free into the world. No longer was it an unspectacular earth-bound caterpillar but a remarkable and dazzling butterfly that gracefully soared through the air with newfound freedom and charm. Now, that's an impressive change!

Imagine yourself as a caterpillar who doesn't believe it'll ever transform into a butterfly. What if I told you that it's only your thoughts of being a failure that are keeping you stuck in that mode? What if all you need to do is unhack your inner programs in order to recognize that you, as a caterpillar and a butterfly, are the same being simply experiencing a different stage of your life?

A caterpillar's perception of self and the outer world is quite different from that of a butterfly. They couldn't be more different. When it is sitting quietly on a tree branch, it is unaware of its potential to fly. But that

potential is still there, hidden, dormant, and waiting for the right time and environment for it to be realized. Even though that potential to fly is innately within the caterpillar, if the caterpillar hasn't experienced it yet and has no awareness of it, it cannot possibly understand the perspective of a butterfly. It has no concept of the beauty of its wings, the ability to fly free, and the vision of the world from a very different point of view.

But a caterpillar doesn't cry about its inability to fly. It doesn't resent the butterfly for its beauty and seeming advantage. Rather, it just goes with the flow of life and allows the metamorphosis to occur without comparing itself to the butterfly or agonizing about the what-ifs. It remains calm during the natural progression and has an unconscious knowing that everything is working according to nature's plan, evolving just as it is designed to. It's as though there is trust in that natural progression of life, with no judgment or expectations of what could or should be.

> It's not that uncommon to perceive yourself
> as a failure when you have self-limiting beliefs.

It's not that uncommon to perceive yourself as a failure when you have self-limiting beliefs. Some of them can show up as you feeling inferior, not enough, not worthy, deserving, or capable. In that way, you are not that different from a caterpillar, as within you lies that dormant potential to become a butterfly, fly free, and enjoy life, recognizing your own beauty and the vastness of the world around you. The caterpillar and the butterfly are the same being, just at different stages and experiencing their reality from a different perspective.

You might find yourself going through life in a perpetual state of feeling like a caterpillar— limited in your view of what's possible and stuck playing small, unaware of your ability to "fly". You may not even be aware that this potential is already within you and always has been. Once you realize that you are the same being who is experiencing life as both the caterpillar and the butterfly, you can begin to understand how to evolve from one stage to the other. It becomes a matter of bringing the unconscious identity to a more conscious awareness of why you live as a "caterpillar" vs. a "butterfly." Then the question is, as both, what makes you associate more with one than the other?

Much of it has to do with your environment, what's familiar, and what you've been conditioned (hacked) to perceive as your reality based on your cultural and familial norms, belief systems, past experiences, and traumas. If all you've ever known are caterpillars, then you do not even know you have the potential to become a butterfly. But even though you do not have that conscious awareness, that potential still lies dormant within you, waiting to awaken.

Sometimes, fear of change keeps you stuck, a defense mechanism that tries to protect you from stepping into the unknown, unfamiliar, and into a different chapter of your life. How often have you seen someone stuck in their unhappy marriage while wondering if there's something or someone better out there, wondering if they can have a happily ever after that they dream of? But instead, they continue to remain stuck because of the many fears directing their actions or inactions.

Or perhaps you might know someone who hates going to work every day, feeling trapped doing the work they do not enjoy, or having a nasty boss who makes them feel unappreciated and taken advantage of. And yet they keep going to that job day after day, frustrated and yet unable or unwilling to try something else. That would require taking a chance, which is a risk, and our egos are not prone to risk-taking actions. But sometimes life gives you a gentle—or not such a gentle—nudge, like that unhappy marriage ending with a spouse leaving them for someone else or that miserable boss firing them.

What do you do with that change in your life, and how do you feel about it? For many of us, our egos have a tough time handling it, even though a part of us knows that we should be happy and thankful. Instead, we end up feeling hurt, abandoned, misled, cheated, etc. To me, this scenario is a perfect moment for some introspection and seeing this crossroads as an opportunity to choose the direction in which your life can go.

Through introspection, you realize you are *not* your thoughts or your feelings. You are the being that has the awareness and ability to experience all of those. There is a way to choose different thoughts, and in doing so, you end up redesigning your life. It's time to change your identity from one of a limited point of view—seeing yourself as small and not enough—to one of a limitless, abundant being, living your most incredible life.

Reality Check

Life happens, and as you make your way through it, your story is created when you experience different events and occasions, and you attach some meaning to them. You then create a story in your mind about what happened to make sense of it. Unconsciously, you label it as a good or bad event. But without that label, it is just the facts about the incident. By labeling the event, you may acquire different beliefs about yourself, such as "I'm unlovable" or "They think I'm a failure." With a story constantly replayed in your mind, on repeat, it's no wonder it begins feeding your thoughts from the beliefs you have formed about yourself or from the opinions of someone else. Your story was invented due to your thoughts being created from an opinion, which then became a belief and led you to accept it as a fact. Once you realize you have done this, you can change it. As the writer of your story, you can start by sorting facts from the fiction you have created from opinions and examine your thought patterns.

Observing and gradually changing these thoughts leads to changing the beliefs around the story that you created. From there, a shift in your emotional state occurs, which in turn changes your energetic vibration. You start to feel better and then behave differently. If you were angry and blaming everyone for your misery, you might find yourself becoming more aware of your emotions and holding yourself accountable for your choices.

Learning to be able to separate the facts about the situation from the labels, how you judge it, and your opinions about it is an important step in expanding your consciousness. As you practice doing so, you find that you can change your perception of a particular scenario and see it in a whole new light. An example of this would be if you were late for your flight and you missed it. This happened to my husband's grandfather. He was waiting for his flight and decided to get a drink at the bar at the airport. Well, he must have had one too many and ended up missing his flight. He took the next flight home and, on arrival, found his wife mourning his loss; the plane he was supposed to be on had gone down.

Most people who missed their flight would likely feel angry, upset, and mad at themselves or someone else. But what if, instead of these negative thoughts, you chose to think differently about it? What if you said to yourself, "Okay, I missed that flight. Perhaps there is a reason for it?" I firmly believe that everything in our lives happens for a reason and for our good, even if we do not know it at the time. I sometimes have to remind myself that the Universe is rigged in my favor. When I accept that, there's an immediate shift in my energy and a push in the state of my overall alignment, leading me to think more positively and be more accepting of what is.

My Rollercoaster Ride

During my teenage years, some significant events impacted my life, which led to me forming certain perceptions about my reality. One major event was when my family and I immigrated to the United States to start a new life. That event in and of itself had no inherent positive or negative implications. I was leaving everything and everyone I knew behind, and it was a time of tremendous stress, unease, and anxiety with the prospect of some potential benefits and disadvantages. Add to that, I was a teenager. Being a teenager can be a difficult period in your life

where your hormones, thoughts, and feelings are all over the place. It was like being on a rollercoaster with the typical ups and downs of adolescence, with the added stress of tremendous uncertainty, not knowing the language, culture, or what the future would hold. However, as I realized later, I unconsciously assigned a lot of negative meaning to what I was experiencing rather than focusing on anything positive during that period of my life. The stories I created surrounding my struggles, difficulties, scarcity, bullying, and health issues became thoughts playing on repeat in my head. Life felt like a major struggle, and during this challenging phase, my energetic vibration was low. I believed life wasn't fair and felt sorry for myself, blaming my circumstances for what I had to endure and wondering why all of that was happening to me.

Little by little, though, I began to realize that life was not happening *to* me, but rather it was happening *for* me. I started to recognize that I was the creator of those stories and, more importantly, that I could choose to create a different story just as easily.

At some point, I saw a very clear connection between my thoughts and how they made me feel. I began to see exactly how those thoughts were like strange magnets, attracting so many more of the same thoughts, which, in turn, were keeping me feeling stuck. I knew it was time to create new thought patterns if I wanted to see a change in my outward reality. I remember, one day, I had an epiphany, a realization that I was not experiencing that same level of anxiety and angst that I normally went to sleep and woke up with daily. I had my first "aha" moment of clarity and a sense of empowerment and joy that I hadn't experienced before. That moment, that realization, was the true beginning of an amazing journey to transformation.

I chose to rewrite my stories into ones of growth and empowerment. Yes, it was a fact I was still an immigrant in a new country; however, I no longer concentrated on the negative parts of that experience. I was now choosing to look at the bigger picture and beginning to see all the positives this experience had brought into my life. This was a turning point for me.

Instead of focusing on all the struggles and hardships, I could see them differently—they were opportunities and possibilities given to me to start a new life, one filled with options that I couldn't have had if I had remained where I was born. I could see the bigger scale of my life journey as it unfolded. I realized there was a deeper meaning and reasons why I had to experience certain things in life in order to grow from them.

> But one day, I met with my college dean who gave me
> some valuable advice that changed everything for me.

My journey has been a rollercoaster of self-discovery and growth. I look back at my younger days and wish someone had told me that it would all work out. I remember how stressed and uncertain I felt when I first started college. I didn't know what I wanted to do with my life and felt lost and unsure of my path. But one day, I met with my college dean who gave me some valuable advice that changed everything for me. She said, "Helen, follow your heart and do what you love. Take classes that make you feel alive and excited. Remember, most people change their career at least twice in their lives, so do not put too much pressure on finding the perfect fit right away."

Her words resonated with me, and I took them to heart. I started taking psychology classes, which I found fascinating, and ended up getting my degree in psychology. Interestingly, I did end up changing my career three times, but the common thread through all of them, as I had realized later, was that they all shared a component of helping others in different capacities.

Throughout the years I was told that I have a knack for connecting people. Funny enough, I introduced five couples that ended up being married. Years later, it all came full circle, and I found my true calling as a healer and relationship coach, helping many long term single people uncover their true selves and break free from their limiting beliefs and old programs so they could open themselves up to love.

My journey has taught me that it's never too late to tap into our passions and that with the right mindset and attitude, we can overcome even the toughest challenges. I am grateful for the lessons and experiences that have led me to where I am today. I feel honored to be able to use my gifts to help others.

Things happened for a reason, even if it took me some time to recognize and accept that. Following that revelation, I have learned to see how each challenging or painful experience in my life acted as a stepping stone guiding me toward the next step and became a catalyst for further growth, knowledge, and expansion. I flipped my thinking and turned my negative point of view about my life experiences into a positive one. Little by little, that became my default way of looking at things.

To be truthful and put things in perspective, I did have those experiences that some would see as difficult or negative. Additionally, I certainly had people around who confirmed and supported my negative beliefs and happily affirmed my victim story, just like that saying goes: "misery loves company." However, I have come to realize that just because I perceived my life a certain way at that time, and there may have been other people in my life agreeing with me and my story, it does not make it the only way to perceive it. Although we all shared similar thoughts and biased opinions about it, we could have easily chosen a different way to look at those things.

During those challenging times, and with the perception I held, I didn't realize that my mind was creating these stories that were keeping me stuck in a particular mindset. Once I recognized the effects of the story I was constantly telling myself, I was finally able to notice my programs and beliefs, observe my thoughts, and eventually, I began to question them. I began to see that I was not a victim of my circumstances; I was a powerful creator of my life experiences and had the power to create a new story. Eventually, I did create a new story, and what a profound difference it has made to my life.

This led to the birth of the STEER Method™, where I could get aspects of my life unstuck, reframe my thought processes and get my life back on track. The STEER Method™ is based on the premise that as you go through life, you tend to assign meaning and judgment to different situations, creating stories in your mind about your experiences based on your perception of the situation. Those stories keep generating similar repeating thoughts, creating beliefs around the interpretation of the story, perpetuating more of the same types of thoughts, which, in turn, continue to reaffirm the story. This ends up triggering an emotional response and physical sensations in the body, and all of it affects your entire energy field, shaping your choices and actions or inaction, which then leads to the results that you attract and experience in your life.

The STEER Method™

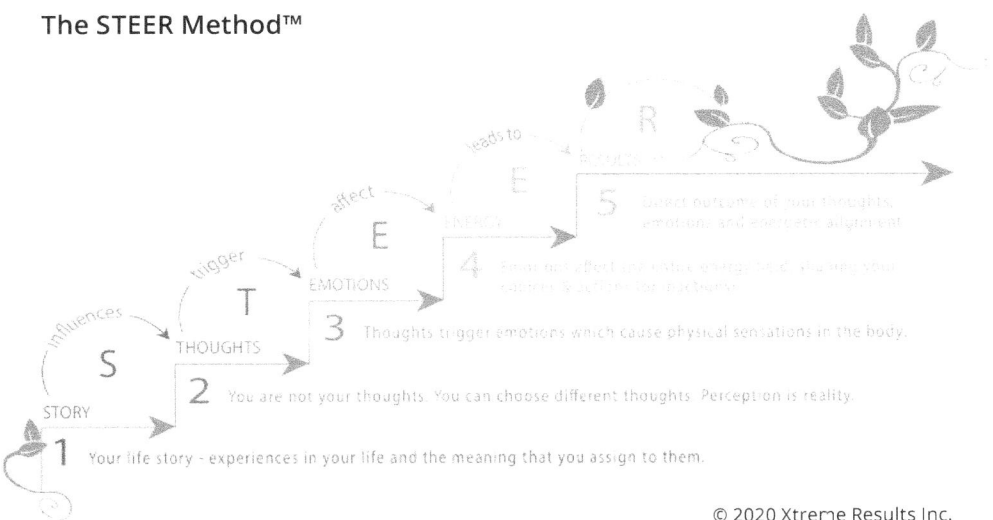

© 2020 Xtreme Results Inc.

I had to change the **Story** I was telling myself and reprogram my thinking, so my **Thoughts** were different, leading to different **Emotions,** creating a shift in my **Energy** and state of being, making me a vibrational match to different people and experiences and creating the desired **Results.** I rewrote my story instead of following the unhealed, unconscious script that I once lived by.

I have seen many methods that promise to deliver the same outcomes, but they are always missing an important component. Some techniques are great at working on your mindset or emotions but completely dismiss the key component of shifting your vibrational energy. Others offer a lot of spirituality but disregard the importance of working on your mental and emotional state. To me, these components are essential. Years ago, when I figured out the missing link, that's when I began to see the biggest shift in every aspect of my life and apply my experience and gifts to help countless others. It is my life's purpose to help heal and elevate the world one person at a time and help them become more fulfilled, happy, and successful in every sphere of their life.

When you use this method, you won't just learn the tools and techniques to improve your life; you can actually apply them and watch your life transform before your eyes. This is the same system I used to create the dream life for myself: transitioning from a poor immigrant with no glimpse of what could be possible to a successful soulpreneur, running a business, living my life's purpose, connected to my authentic self and bringing value to the world while enjoying my personal life as a wife, mom, sister, daughter, and friend.

It was not easy and didn't happen overnight. It took me many years of continuous learning, struggling, and working on myself to gradually create a deep shift at the identity level. If only I'd known then what I know now… But again, I believe there is a deeper reason behind this journey of self-discovery.

The more I learned to connect the dots between what I was thinking and the way I was feeling, the more I was able to question my beliefs and thoughts and rewrite my stories. And as though by magic, everything in my life began to shift. Suddenly, more and more opportunities began to align, synchronicities started to occur regularly, and the right people were coming across my path to support the new belief system based on new thoughts and new stories. The more I studied the mind-body connection, learning about vibrational energy and the various healing modalities, the more I not just saw the connection but actually noticed how much more joyous, fulfilling, and in the flow my life was beginning to feel.

As I briefly mentioned above, I had many health issues growing up, and these affected my reality. The narrative given to me was "It's all in your head," "You are a hypochondriac," "There is nothing wrong, that pain is not real, here are some psychiatric meds," and on and on. I had a choice—either I continued living someone else's beliefs or started living my own truth. Unconsciously, I began unhacking myself; I had no choice but to seek my own healing. When I did, it turned out that it was *not* all in my head. It was just that the medical system did not have the answers that would fit within their box. So, I learned to look and think outside the box. I learned how to heal at the root and work on finding solutions rather than chasing symptoms.

For me, healing and unhacking myself has been a journey of self-discovery: learning to trust my inner guidance and seek answers and solutions even when so called experts say there are none. I embarked on a pilgrimage of unhacking myself to break away from needing validation from outside sources, to face my shadows, and to heal my inner child—one of self-acceptance and self-love. Imagine what your life would be like if you unhacked yourself and let go of all that heavy emotional baggage you've been carrying.

Whether it be your marriage, career, financial success or your health, it's time to unhack yourself from the cycle of helplessness and misery you've been programmed to believe and start reframing your story.

> It's time to take control of the steering wheel of your life. It's time to Unhack Yourself.

Whether you realize it or not, your brain is a supercomputer operating at an amazingly high level, and it is able to be reprogrammed. It has been receiving data throughout your life and is capable of amazing things. However, sometimes, that data has been compromised or hacked during your life's journey, which can cause your mind to run false programs that prevent you from performing at your optimum level. Perhaps you may feel like your life is not moving in the direction it should. Perhaps it's not moving at all, and you are feeling stuck. Maybe you feel bogged down in a thankless or dreary job where showing up is a daily chore. Maybe you are seeking a more satisfying and fulfilling life. It's possible that your relationships never turn out to be the happily-ever-after you imagined, and you feel wounded and

hurt, time after time. It's time to take control of the steering wheel of your life. It's time to Unhack Yourself.

Of course, healing your life and unhacking yourself is possible, but I want to warn you it is a journey that takes time and effort. It is a process that requires being open to new perspectives and possibilities. It involves a willingness to change and be in touch with your thoughts, emotions and energy around situations in your life where there's frustration, pain, anger, fear, and a lack of control. Instead, you get to create a reality where you attract from your true worth rather than your wounds. Think of your return to your natural default state, free from all the stories, traumas, pains, and faulty programs, as a reset to your original factory setting. It's like having an entire system reboot, with the added bonus of having virus and malware protection. You will have the lifelong tools and ability to Unhack Yourself for good.

My goal for you is to become more conscious, more connected, and more aware of your current paradigm and to share ways for you to change it. This book is a gateway to help you gain an awareness of:

- *Your unconscious blocks (and they can be sneaky!)*

- *How those blocks affect your life and current reality*

- *How to get back into the driver's seat of your life*

- *How to have the self-confidence and be able to access tools that will help you take the next step in activating and achieving your goals*

I want you to be less stressed while achieving more than you ever thought possible. This book will serve as a guide for you along your path. It is designed for you to develop the skills you need to create a life that enables you to soar like a butterfly.

Are you prepared for the journey?

At the center of your being, you have the answer; you know who you are, and you know what you want.

Lao Tzu

Discovering Who and Where You Are

When I think about the question, "Who are you?" I automatically think of Lewis Carroll's *Alice's Adventures in Wonderland* and the caterpillar who repeatedly asks this of Alice. He didn't ask this question to confuse her; he wanted her to look deeper into herself and recognize her potential. To do this, Alice had to recognize *where* she was and what her purpose was.

You have likely asked yourself similar questions. It's important that you play the parts of the caterpillar and Alice when they arise. Do not stop asking (the caterpillar) or looking for answers (Alice). (Here's a hint: The answers often shift.) As you journey through Part One, you will start to formulate answers, which is the start of you becoming the hero of your story.

Like the sun, the inner self is always shining, but because of negative clouds, we do not experience it. It is not necessary to program oneself with the truth; it is only necessary to remove that which is false.

Sir David R. Hawkins, M.D., PH.D.

CHAPTER ONE

Being a Conscious Observer

once heard a Buddhist story about a man walking on a long journey through life. As he's walking, the dirt from the road sticks to him. The farther he walks, the more he gets covered by layer upon layer of dirt. After a short time, we can no longer see the man underneath the dirt, and sadly, the man himself starts to identify as that dirt. Unfortunately, he'd forgotten that this surface layer of dirt was not actually him.

> I always found it fascinating to see how many people
> go through life so deeply programmed to believe
> that they are somehow broken and need to be fixed.
> But the truth is, *you were never broken.*

This story resonated with me deeply, as I have always been a curious observer of life. I always found it fascinating to see how many people go through life so deeply programmed to believe that they are somehow broken and need to be fixed. But the truth is, *you were never broken.* Just like the man in this story, you need to remove the layers of what's false, peel away all the layers of the acquired proverbial dirt—the false identity you acquired through your past experiences and sometimes passed on through generations.

Choosing Our Lens

I had the privilege of guiding a client through the transformative journey of shedding false layers of identity as she worked persistently to manifest her

soulmate over the course of many years. She had dated different men throughout the years but never had a real connection with anyone. After we cleared numerous layers of stuck energy, unprocessed emotions since early childhood, and even some generational trauma patterns she'd inherited and unknowingly carried for years, she finally met someone.

We discussed her blossoming relationship in one of our sessions after they had met. This man was almost shockingly exactly what she'd described to me numerous times during our work together. I do not mean his looks, even though he matched her description in that arena too. What I found surprising is to what extent precisely every element about him was what she thought she wanted in a man.

We continued clearing more layers of looting beliefs, self-sabotaging patterns, and the energetic shield protecting her heart from getting hurt. One day, she confided to me that she had begun to question whether or not this man's personality traits were what she truly wanted. She began to wonder if she manifested the "wrong" person. And that's when it dawned on me: When she was initially working on manifesting this man, she was working from her old paradigm of thoughts, emotions, and energetic vibration.

Her energy began shifting as we cleared more and more of those layers. She started to see things differently, from the perspective of a less-wounded person whose heart was now more open to giving and receiving love. It's not that this guy was suddenly wrong for her; it's that she began to perceive him through a different lens. Think of it this way: She was living in darkness and perceived life through a well-developed night vision. As we began to turn the light on little by little, the same things and people she saw through that dark lens began to get illuminated. When you shed some light on things, they tend to appear slightly different.

Once you gain this awareness and unhack your mind of the story you've had playing on repeat, you can consciously choose how you want to move forward. In this client's case, she realized that while this man she truly manifested matched her unhealed version's desires, he also offered a journey of continued self-growth. Through loving him, she began to truly know herself and understand her deepest pains, true value, and soul's lessons.

There Is No Try

I have seen countless people searching for a deeper connection with themselves and the world in order to truly understand themselves. They want to live with more purpose and joy and reach their full potential. One of the essential lessons I have learned is the power of letting go of "trying."

> The concept of trying has a negative connotation to it,
> as it implies there is a potential you may not succeed.

You may have been taught that success comes from hard work and perseverance. But the truth is, this belief can hold you back. The concept of trying has a negative connotation to it, as it implies there is a potential you may not succeed. So, when you say, "I'm trying," it implies you know there is a possibility of not accomplishing it. In a way, you unknowingly set yourself up for failure. This negative energy can block you from manifesting what you want.

In *Feel Free to Prosper*, Marilyn Jennett explains that the harder you try something, the less chance you have of achieving it. It's similar to what Yoda from *Star Wars* says: "Do or do not, there is no try." This means you must approach your goals with confidence and commitment. By being present in the moment and taking action, you can bring your desires to life. So the next time you hear yourself say, "I am trying," I urge you to notice it and replace the trying with "I am doing it," or "I am working on or toward it." And notice how different those statements feel.

Unlocking a New Perspective

Let's face it—we've all had our share of disappointments in life and unexpected plot twists in our personal stories. However, it's often not the disappointments that leave you feeling crushed; it's how you let them lodge deep within you. From this internal space, your emotions can allow misery and anguish to take hold, and you often unknowingly permit them to dictate the trajectory of your day-to-day life. Those emotional responses to disappointments and setbacks stem from a perceived disconnection, a feeling of separation from your essence. Consider how your disappointing experiences have also contributed to your perception and expectations; you may have created a narrow, limited view of your future based on your past observations and experiences. It's as though you unconsciously labeled yourself as damaged, shattered to pieces by every heartbreak and painful experience. Those traumas and wounds hacked your inner beliefs about yourself and created internal stories based on self-limiting beliefs. You are left feeling fragmented, broken, and seeking wholeness. What would happen if you broadened your view?

> The more fear I felt, the less trust or faith I felt, and the more
> my self-confidence was diminished, thus creating a void,
> a mental gap, a separation from the present moment.

For years, I suffered from debilitating anxiety and panic attacks. As I progressed in my healing journey, I realized a ruptured connection with what some would call God or the Universe, or what I call the Inner Self, triggered my anxiety. The more fear I felt, the less trust or faith I felt, and the more my self-confidence was diminished, thus creating a void, a mental gap, a separation from the present moment. My mind would quickly concoct all sorts of "what-if" scenarios, which would usually be quite scary and generally much worse than reality.

During that time, I heard Dr. Wayne Dyer explain, "If you change the way you look at things, the things you look at change." I began to shift my focus from the fear-based stories and ruminating on the negative thoughts and the bodily responses they were creating to concentrating on being more mindful and staying in the present, observing rather than judging. I diligently worked on clearing layer upon layer of the unresolved emotional big and small traumas and experiences that left me feeling fragmented or broken in some way. This resulted in calmness and a feeling of being whole and connected.

Your expanded perspective starts by evaluating the story you are telling yourself and the thoughts and emotions that arise from that narrative. It's important to bring awareness of that negativity and shift it into positive ways of being in order to achieve what you want. Remember, you are not your thoughts; you are the thinker, the being behind all your thoughts, and you have the ability to change them.

Your fears and expectations of disappointment and unworthiness have been clouding your ability to see the potential in yourself and others, while your past thoughts and thinking patterns have created everything in your life right now. If you'd like to see any changes in your life, the first step is to change your thoughts to correspond and align with your goals. Once you realize that all the limitations are created only in your mind, you can start to create a change in your life and upgrade your software—you can start on the path of awakening. Nothing outside of yourself prevents you from having success, happiness, and joy in your life. There is no lack of opportunities other than the lack of limiting beliefs in your mind.

Erasing limiting beliefs one by one creates a state of mind that becomes like a magnet to opportunities for success, financial abundance, the right people and situations, and existing as truly awakened.

Here's a quick exercise to complete before you continue on.

Use the chart below to create a wish list of two or three things you want to achieve and give yourself a specific timeframe. It may be helpful to list a large goal, like landing your dream job, then drill down into smaller, more easily completed achievements that will bring you closer to the big one. Make sure you are not putting "counter-wishes" in your list. (This is something like wishing to be healthy when you are not sick.)

Achievement	Timeframe
Write a novel (big goal)	1 year
—Write the first chapter (sub-goal)	1 month

Once you get what you want, make sure to remove it from your list. Keeping track of your goals like this will help you to replace your limiting beliefs (i.e., I could never write a novel) and bring you closer to becoming your awakened self.

Erasing limiting beliefs one by one creates a state of mind that becomes like a magnet to opportunities for success, financial abundance, and the right people and situations.

Self-Reflection

You have the ability to shape your thoughts, thereby molding life according to your perspective and choices. As you already know, your reality is a reflection of your perception. It is the story you have created that influences your thoughts. That is where the "T" in the STEER Method™ comes in and focuses on your thoughts. You may struggle with constant negative thoughts, making you interpret your reality as stuck or less than what you desire. Those constantly repeating thoughts create beliefs around your interpretation of the story, and unfortunately, you end up perpetuating more of the same types of thoughts. In turn, this keeps affirming the Story. Negativity leads to more negativity. But when you focus on positive thoughts, you send a message to the Universe that you are open and ready to receive all the good things you desire. It creates a vibration of positivity that shifts your energy to attract abundance and happiness.

So many people carry a heavy burden of guilt, shame, anger, resentment, jealousy, and other negative feelings and emotions often directed at people very close to them and sometimes directly at themselves. Interestingly, once you become a conscious observer of human behavior and emotions, it often becomes

quite obvious how certain behaviors and thinking patterns keep creating the life you are living and the situations you encounter. You probably know someone who carries some anger, guilt, or blame. How can you manifest a loving, happy world for yourself if your vibration aligns with those negative emotions?

In my practice, I have observed a consistent pattern among clients throughout the years—a pervasive absence of self-love that seems to be a shared struggle for so many people. How can you be truly happy without loving yourself? One of the most powerful quotes about love comes from Byron Katie: "Do you want to meet the love of your life? Look in a mirror." One of the ways to practice self-love is often referred to as mirror work, where you look in the mirror and experience loving the person you see, flaws and all. Louise Hay, who has been the biggest catalyst in my healing journey, has done a lot of work on this topic. She said, "Because the mirror reflects back to you the feelings you have about yourself. It makes you immediately aware of where you are resisting and where you are open and flowing. It clearly shows you what thoughts you will need to change if you want to have a joyous, fulfilling life." I use this technique in The STEER Method™ because it uncovers the areas of resistance. Your success ceiling in any sphere of your life is your own beliefs about it.

I like to treat life as a giant playground. I throw the ball of thoughts and feelings matched with an energetic vibration at the Universe and allow it to throw it right back to me. The game is on. Be warned, though; this is not a competition. If you try to play against the Universe, you will lose the game every time.

Let go of trying. Believe in yourself and your abilities.
Have fun with it, surrender to the laws of the Universe,
and allow it to play with you. Always remember:
The Universe is rigged in *your* favor.

As you journey through your day and healing experience, it's important to remain a conscious observer of your thoughts, emotions, and (re)actions. How is your perspective creating the stories in your mind? How can you shift your perspective and rewrite the story? It's okay not to have the answers to those questions now. As you continue through this book, the answers will become clearer. Soon, you'll truly be the conscious author of your story.

*Intuition is a very powerful thing,
more powerful than intellect.*

Steve Jobs

CHAPTER TWO

Beyond Logic:
The Power of Intuition

I f you have been around children or can remember your childhood, you know they perceive the world differently than adults. "I'm going to be a superhero when I grow up!" "Do not step on cracks, or you'll break your mother's back." "I'm going to live on Mars." You probably hear these things as an adult, and your logical mind discounts the possibilities. You decide they are not real and cannot happen. But what if kids have it right? When logic starts to overwrite the "childish programming," you get stuck in a robotic state of doing while losing touch with your intuition—your ability to "know" over what you are programmed to believe.

Your intuition is your connection to your soul essence.

One of the biggest ways you have been hacked is how you were taught to rely on your logic and disregard your intuition, which, in reality, has always been your biggest gift. Your intuition is your connection to your soul essence. When you ignore it, you only rely on your perception of what you see, which has been hacked to begin with (I hope you are starting to see the bigger picture).

It's no wonder humans live in a state of stress and overwhelm. How can you not be when you are disconnected from your true self? You are taught to work hard, hustle, achieve, and constantly look for validation of

success in something outside of yourself. So, you live in a perpetual state of chasing and never having enough, which, in turn, leaves an unconscious sense of feeling that you are never enough.

In contrast, unhacking and liberating yourself from mental constraints allows you to be guided by and place trust in your inner wisdom. It's like being led by an invisible hand that always knows the right direction. There is no need to struggle; instead, just surrender and be guided. You begin to live in the flow of life rather than resisting the current. So much of people's stress, anxiety, and unhappiness is caused by feeling disconnected, which stems from being detached from your inner essence. Your logical mind, driven by the ego's need to be right or to have a sense of control, rationalizes your way through life. It develops creative stories while searching for your purpose in life. Those stories attempt to justify why you choose to do what you do, i.e., it's a great career, it's secure, you'll always have a job, you'll never go hungry, he's a good guy, she'll make a good wife, etc.

Society teaches you to think your way out of problems and look for solutions. The issue with that is when you strictly rely on your logic and ignore your heart and intuition—or your stories give you a different perspective of what seems to make sense logically—often you find yourself in a great job or career that pays well, but you hate it or become stuck in unfulfilling relationships that seemed like a good decision at the time.

But did you know that thinking about and focusing on the problem perpetuates the problem? If you want to find a solution, you need to do what seems counterintuitive—try to forget about the problem and instead focus on what's going well in your life and the outcome you want to experience. As your focus shifts, the problem eventually will resolve or cease to be a problem. Why not try it and see for yourself?

Focusing on the problem
perpetuates the problem.

There is a way to connect with that inner knowing—to harness the power you possess and your intuition to guide you to make the right decision every time. The more you listen to and act on intuitive nudges, the more you'll begin to experience living in the flow instead of in a state of constant struggle with life. Synchronicities will show up in your life. That's when you begin to operate beyond the conscious mind, which can feel like magic sometimes.

You'll begin dismantling the limiting beliefs and stories that kept you stuck for so long and may suddenly find yourself seeing things in a new light. You'll start to see new opportunities and abundance and meet new people that you never imagined possible before. Gradually, you'll learn to trust your intuition. That's when real magic enters your life.

When you trust your intuition, you gain more confidence in yourself. You eliminate the self-doubt, experience an increased sense of inner peace and calm, and finally heal and reclaim parts of yourself that you may have written off as permanently damaged. By connecting to your intuition, you learn to expand your energetic capacity to start experiencing higher levels of prosperity, abundance, and success in all areas of life.

Be confident and do not give in to fear; it suppresses your intuition and lowers your energetic frequency. Elevate yourself and activate your intuition to finally live on your terms. Remember, you do not get what you want; you get what you vibrate.

Connecting With Your Intuitive Guidance

When your intuitive guidance is activated, it usually comes in fast, like lightning, and often goes unnoticed as a fleeting feeling that shows up briefly and then disappears or quickly gets taken over by the rational mind. Think of it this way: When you take a multiple-choice exam, the exam giver often advises you to go with the first answer that comes to mind. When you try to correct it, it's usually the wrong answer. The reason is that when logic and reasoning take over, it suppresses the initial gut feeling, which is always right. The mind operates on logic. which is often fear- or lack-based, and blocks the intuitive answer that comes first.

Being aligned with your inner truth means you no longer need to seek external validation. You are guided by your intuition and live in a heart-centered space, which is infinitely bigger than the world of pure logic and thoughts. You live in a state of surrender to the flow of life rather than struggling against the current.

Emotions and energy play important roles in learning to harness your intuition. As the STEER Method™ teaches, those two aspects go hand in hand. Allowing your emotions to run away with your negative story and thoughts lowers your energetic vibration and effectively blocks your intuition. In contrast, embracing positive emotions increases your energetic vibration, allowing your intuition to guide you.

So, how do you develop this intuition, expand your energetic vessel, and raise your vibration? I have an entire course on this topic, but I'd love to share some of my favorite tips and techniques to help you start connecting to yourself.

Here are my top tips to help you develop your inner guidance:

Develop Your Inner Guidance

- **Practice trusting your intuition** by connecting to people by what you feel, not what you see. Energy doesn't lie! People can lie with their words and actions but not with their energy.
- **Start to look at every experience** with a sense of curiosity rather than judgment.
- **Pay attention to the feeling in your body.** When feeling inspired, listen extra carefully. It's likely a sign to move forward with something vs. feeling tightness in your chest or stomach, which can be a major warning sign to steer clear.
- **Notice your underlying beliefs about your reality.** Do you believe the Universe is rigged in your favor? Or do you resonate more with the thinking that the Universe laughs at your expense? The first belief system is conducive to growth and expansion, whereas the other blocks your inner guidance and success.
- **Detox your body,** feed it high-vibrational foods, and drink more water. When your body is toxic, your intuitive guidance feels unclear.
- **Connect to nature.** Walk barefoot on the ground or the beach or hug a tree for a minute with your eyes closed. Notice the energy shifting throughout your body.

Intuitive guidance can come as a chance remark from someone, a song on the radio, or a sign on the road. Become more aware of the signs and welcome them. The more you accept them, the more you'll receive. (We talk more about reading these signs in the next chapter.)

If you truly want to connect to your inner guidance, you must accept it and be grateful it's there. Then, you have to tune into it. The more you attune yourself to it, the more it becomes second nature, and eventually, inner guidance happens automatically.

How can you connect with your intuition? Here are some steps to help.

Connect With Your Intuition

1. **Become vulnerable.** Acknowledge that you are okay with the way you are and allow yourself to become open to tapping into your intuition. You often ignore your intuition speaking to you. The main key to expanding it is actually learning to accept it, to respect it, and then expect it.

2. **Be aware of your feelings and emotions.** Does a particular person or situation make you feel constricted, closed off, or uncomfortable? Or is it making you feel more expansive and open like your breath is free vs. constricted?

3. **Muscle testing.** This is a powerful tool I use and teach my clients that helps connect to and communicate with your unconscious so you can get answers from your higher self rather than your logical mind. Sometimes, it serves as a great lie detector, as your body doesn't lie; it always shares the truth and innately knows what's good or bad for you. This tool can give you access to answers beyond the logical mind and guide you to the right choices, no matter how big or small. I have used it pretty much in every area of my life. Whether it's a question of what food item to pick from the menu, what vitamin would benefit you or whether this house or job is the right one for you, once you access it and learn to utilize it, it becomes your best friend for life.

4. **Free your mind.** Whenever you are working under stress or pressure, you are disconnected from your intuition. So, in order to connect to it, get quiet and allow yourself to be present with no distractions. It never comes from being forced or under pressure. My favorite time to do this is when I'm falling asleep or just waking up.

5. **Shut off your logical mind.** Logic will try to suppress intuition. Intuition is having a deep inner knowing. It goes far beyond the conscious level of thought and logic.

6. **Trust yourself.** When you learn to trust yourself rather than constantly looking for validation from the outside world, you begin to rely on your feelings. You shift into having a deep sense of knowing.

When you live based on intuition, you stop relying on the idea of "OMG, I need to make a decision. What's the right decision? What if I make a wrong one?" In this frame of mind, you try to control the outcome and avoid what you would perceive as a negative outcome. The alternative way of living is by following your intuitive guidance.

I'm constantly tuned into my inner guidance. Let me share an experience where this guidance was so crazy it was hard to believe. It was when my husband and I were looking to buy a new house. A few years into our journey, we had thought about giving up on the idea because the house I visualized, and the price point we could afford did not seem to exist. But I knew the right one would be ours when the divine timing was right.

During this time, I was studying feng shui. According to Chinese beliefs, the number four is unlucky because "four" and "death" sound similar in Chinese. So, each time a house with the number four in the address came on the market, I didn't bother to visit it because I knew that this belief of it being unlucky would bother me to no end.

We checked the real estate listings daily and patiently waited. One evening, my husband called me to come quickly and look at the new home listing that had just come out. I laughed and told him I had already seen all the listings for that day. (I always did this first thing in the morning when they posted all the new listings.) But he insisted, so I walked into the office, glanced at the computer screen, and stared in disbelief. At just one glance, I knew it would be our new home.

As my husband read the description and showed me more pictures, that feeling inside me grew stronger and stronger. It was the one. But then he quietly said to me, "Hon, you won't believe it; it's number four."

My heart sank. Thoughts and questions started racing through my mind. I knew my feelings couldn't be wrong. I trusted it one hundred percent, but I also knew myself, and that belief in the unluckiness of the number four would bother me immensely. So, I went to sleep, thinking I'd have a better answer in the morning.

The following morning started with a call from our realtor, who had been so patient and had kept working with us for over a year after other realtors gave up and said our dream home didn't exist. I picked up and said, "Hi, I'm surprised you didn't call me last night."

She laughed and said, "So, you already know why I'm calling? When do you want to go see this house?"

We agreed to meet at the house an hour before I left for work.

When I walked into that house, I just knew I was home. I have never had such a strong feeling of knowing before. As we walked from room to room, I felt like I already knew where everything was. While touring the house, I told my realtor we were prepared to make an offer. She was surprised to hear that my husband, already at work, didn't need to see the house. When we looked at it online the night before, we knew it was the one. It had everything we envisioned for more than two years and at the price we could afford - except for the small, but not so small, number four.

So, I debated with myself. On the one hand, I knew this house was definitely "the one," and even that number wouldn't stop me. But on the other hand, I knew myself and knew it would bother me. As I left the house and headed to work, I proclaimed loudly, "God, Universe, please give me a sign." I drove for a while, my mind flooded with thoughts, not noticing anything around me.

Suddenly, my mind returned to the present and I noticed the small truck driving in front of me: it had a small number four on the bottom of its back panel. Above it, there was a large number four next to a picture of a king with a crown on his head, and right above it, in large letters, it said: "Go With the King." I narrowed my eyes, reading it over and over. I couldn't believe what a powerful message I had received. (Amusing side note: The truck belonged to a plumbing company called King Plumbing.)

I thanked the guides and erased all my doubt: it was the right house for me and my family, and everything worked out perfectly. As I said, the Universe has a funny way of sending messages. Some might say I got lucky, but I will say, "You do not get lucky; you make lucky."

Developing Your Intuitive Muscle

Sometimes, it's hard to connect to your intuition, as you have probably been taught your whole life to rely on logic and trust what you have been told by someone else's teachings. In some ways, we have all been indoctrinated to trust authority, such as teachers, parents, religious leaders, and doctors, to name a few. From early on, you learned to ignore your intuition and your inner knowing and just rely on the acquired knowledge and in doing so, you unconsciously have given away your power, your intuitive knowing of what's best for you. Those authority figures you entrusted your knowledge and health to are all human too and, as such, can make mistakes. That's why it's so important to connect to your inner wisdom that always knows the right choice for you. So, how do you flip the switch and learn to rely on your intuition?

First, and this is an extremely important point, stop resisting what your intuition wants to tell you. It often won't be what your logical mind wants to hear, and that's okay. Your thinking mind might create a story that may not be the truth. If something feels like "Oh, I really should be doing this," but all the justifying for why you should be choosing that comes up, that's not intuition. That is your logical mind trying to control you. Be aware: These justifications and beliefs may not be your own.

It's not easy becoming open to receiving intuitive
guidance, but the gut feeling doesn't lie.

It's not easy becoming open to receiving intuitive
guidance, but the gut feeling doesn't lie. The best way
to develop your intuition is to trust it more. Become
okay with *not knowing* and allow it to come. The more
you make peace with trusting rather than relying on
knowledge, the more your intuitive muscle develops.

Creating an Energetic Shift and Realigning Your Frequency

As your intuitive muscle develops, you will be able to
work towards raising your energetic vibration and
creating an energetic shift. Think of your energy as your
bank account. And just like in a bank, people cannot
withdraw from your energy account without your
permission. The people in your life are either depositing
in your energy account or making withdrawals.

What you might not realize, though, is that
permission may not be a conscious one. Until you
bring it to your awareness, you might find a lot of
withdrawals (drained energy) taking place.

How do you create an energetic shift?

First, you need to bring awareness to what energy
frequency you align with that you have unknowingly
accepted as a part of your identity. Then, it's
important to create a pattern interrupt to become
an energetic match to the identity that aligns with
your new intentions.

So often, you create patterns in your life when it
comes to money, relationships, jobs, success, and living
situations, and you find yourself asking, "How the heck

did this happen again?" I have definitely lived as a victim of my circumstances, but I have also realized that dwelling on the could've, should've, and would've was keeping me stuck in the same toxic patterns.

Instead of dwelling on being in victim mode, identify areas that need improvement and create an action plan to make those areas better. After you make improvements, it's important to strengthen your intuition muscle and further elevate your energetic frequency.

Do this daily cleansing routine:

- **Daily Emotional Clearing.** Check in with yourself daily before you go to bed, and let go of any frustrations and negative feelings you have experienced throughout the day. Clear away your emotional toxins.

- **Physical Detox.** When your body is toxic, it blocks your intuition. Eating high-vibrational foods, drinking chlorophyll, using essential oils, and getting sunlight will benefit you and your connection to your inner guidance.

- **Honor and Be Grateful for Any Signs You are Receiving.** Become open to seeing and hearing signs everywhere and respect them by following the intuitive guidance.

- **Adjust How You Look at Things.** Start to look at every experience with a sense of curiosity and a knowing that the Universe is rigged in your favor rather than thinking that it laughs at your expense.

- **Embrace Your Positivity.** This might seem counterintuitive, but rather than feeling less negative, recognize that you are feeling more positive.

- **Connect to Your Intuitively-Guided Feelings.** The tight feeling in your chest or stomach is a major sign to be aware of. When feeling inspired, listen extra carefully—it's a sign to move forward with something. Allow your decision-making to come from that place rather than the unnecessary self-induced stress arising from not knowing the right or wrong decision. Go with the feeling!

- **Laughter as Emotional Medicine.** In the late 1970s, Norman Cousins wrote Anatomy of an Illness as Perceived by the Patient based on his creation of laughter therapy to self-treat his ailments. Laughing helps shift your vibration by flooding your brain with feel-good chemicals (the natural ones, not pharma-made). So, when you feel your energy depleting, take time to watch something that makes you laugh.

- **Gossip Creates Low Vibration.** Gossip is prevalent in so many facets of life. Think about the proverbial water cooler talk. Or look at your social media stream and notice how much of it is gossip and hearsay. Participating in this shifts your energy, resulting in lower vibration. Notice your words, thoughts, beliefs, and focus. You are, after all, what you believe, say, and think.

- **Alter Your Physical Environment.** There is a lot of research on your physical environment and your mental state. While some argue that clutter is a sign of creativity, others point out that clutter overstimulates your brain. According to *Psychology Today,* "Decluttering increases self-worth, creates healthy habits and boosts productivity. A clean and tidy home can also improve sleep, boost mood, and promote relaxation."[1] Decluttering can also shift your energy and improve your intuition. Whether you feel your space is tidy or not, shifting your decor or the colors in your environment can boost your positive energy shift. Try placing items that speak to you spiritually, like crystals or art or adding calming colors like blues and greens.

- **Be Aware of Your Energy Alignment.** Be mindful of your own energy as well as who you surround yourself with. Aligning yourself with people vibrating at a higher energy level will raise yours.

The higher you elevate your vibrational frequency, the easier you can manifest.

---

1   Diane Roberts Stoler, "The Many Mental Benefits of Decluttering," *Psychology Today,* February 15, 2023, https://www.psychologytoday.com/intl/blog/the-resilient-brain/202302/the-many-mental-benefits-of-decluttering#:~:text=Research%20has%20shown%20that%20people,be%20a%20challenge%20for%20anyone.

If you are on the fence about something, listen carefully to your intuition. Could it be trying to tell you something while your thinking mind tries to persuade you to do or not do it? If you want your intuition to override those thoughts, it's important to honor it. One way to do this is by keeping a journal of all your intuitive insights, which also helps you develop your intuitive muscles further.

So, before you go to bed tonight, write down all the moments you noticed your intuition. It's time to break through your inner resistance!

Signs and symbols rule the world,
not words nor laws.

Confucius

CHAPTER THREE

Learn to Read the Signs

Being open to seeing and understanding signs is similar to listening to and accepting your intuitive guidance. Signs are prevalent around you, but you have to be open to seeing them and receptive to their meaning. There is an interesting phenomenon: When you look for something, you'll find it. For example, have you ever bought a car and suddenly started seeing the same vehicle as yours on the road? It's not that you manifest more of those vehicles into existence; you are simply more in tune with that type because it's in the forefront of your subconscious. Depending on how you interpret the sign of seeing more vehicles like yours, you may see this as a positive or negative sign.

As you progress through this chapter, you will explore how your emotions around these signs affect your energy and actions (or inactions).

Number Synchronicities

One of the ways I receive messages from the Universe is through numbers. At times, the way those messages come through seems almost magical.

Do you ever repeatedly see the same number pattern, day after day? Or maybe you've heard someone say, "It's 11:11. Make a wish!" I can't recall when I first heard that as a young girl, but that message stuck with me. From then onward, whenever I saw 11:11, I would make a wish. It seemed silly at first, but it started to seem pretty real after a while when it felt like my wishes were coming true. The feeling was invigorating. Perhaps you have experienced it, too?

At that time, I knew nothing about the Law of Attraction, spirituality, or energetic vibrations. (Those conversations weren't a part of my surroundings until I was much older.) Some part of me, however, innately knew there was a bigger force making things happen, more than I could see with my limited thinking mind.

> As I got older, I started to notice all the synchronicities happening to me and around me.

As I got older, I started to notice all the synchronicities happening to me and around me. At first, I simply acknowledged them, but after a while, it became almost like a game. I accepted and welcomed them into my life. That's when more and more signs started flooding in. I began to rely more on my sixth sense and the messages sent to me from the Universe (or what some people prefer to call from your spirit guides).

An interesting story I want to share with you is something that happened several years ago that was really quite a fascinating and eye-opening experience in manifesting. I decided to look for a condo to use for vacationing. As I was looking, one caught my attention because of its number: 1122. It's not that it was the best condo we've seen. But something about it felt right and the number tied to it alerted my intuition that it was meant to be mine.

For over two decades, I have had a phone number ending with 1122. I wasn't necessarily conscious of it for a long time. However, those numbers have been my biggest signs over the last decade since I became more in tune with my intuition and inner guidance. Any combination of those numbers and my intuition kicks into high gear.

I intuitively asked my subconscious repeatedly and kept getting the answer that it was my condo. So, I went to my husband and declared, "This is going to be our condo. I know it's a significantly higher price than what we can afford. But I know it's meant to be ours. I kept energy-testing the price I would get it for, even though it was significantly lower than the listing price. He replied, "You must be crazy! What are you talking about? There's no way they'll accept our offer."

So we submitted an offer, and the sellers immediately declined. We gave another offer, which they also refused. A few weeks passed, and the realtor returned and said, "Helen, I'm sorry. Another buyer came in. The condo is under contract. It's not your condo."

Naturally, my husband, who is always the first to doubt, said, "See, I told you. Your intuition stuff doesn't work. There's no such thing as intuition." (He's always the skeptic, which is a fun dynamic.)

I replied, "I don't know how or why, but I know what I'm feeling."

It's a feeling that you just tune into. You know when something is meant for you and do not know why. You stop questioning it and accept it because it's your inner knowing.

So, I was very confused. I couldn't explain why the condo was sold to someone else. My entire being said it was mine.

Two or three months later, we went on a vacation after putting the condo-buying experience on the back burner. During the trip, I got a call from the realtor. "Helen, do you remember that condo 1122?"

Of course, I did. "Yes, why?"

"Do you still want it? The deal fell through."

I was astonished. "What do you mean?"

"Well," he began, "it was a corporate buyer from out of the country. The board declined the sale at the last minute. So, it's going to be back on the market. If you still want it, this is your opportunity to come in with your offer because the seller is really motivated to sell it now."

Guess who got the condo and at the price we could afford?

My husband was dumbfounded.

So you could be like my husband, pushing aside your intuition for the logic telling you no. Or you can just trust your inner guidance and have patience. Even though I'm a very logical and practical person, I'm very cognizant of the fact that there are things that surpass logic and practicality.

Another time, I was driving and thinking about a health issue that was starting to worry me and cause lots of anxiety. I was becoming consumed with thinking about it and unsure what to do. Driving has always been my time in a quiet space with no one bothering me, so I asked the Universe for a sign.

After a few minutes, I glanced at my speedometer and saw fifty-five. Okay, I thought, this could be a sign if only it had another five. Frustrated, I exclaimed, "Seriously, couldn't you at least show me another five?" Then, as I was about to turn and looked to my right, I saw a speed limit sign I'd never noticed in all the years of driving on the same road. SPEED LIMIT - FIVE. And just like that, I received my third five—the exact sign I asked to receive.

Numbers are just one of the ways the Universe sends you guiding signs, but it seems like something people have paid attention to throughout the centuries. For example, the fear of the number thirteen (triskaidekaphobia) has persisted in modern Western Civilization through the omission of this number, including many high-rise buildings omitting it in the numbering of floors.[2] Many people believe seeing this number is a sign of bad luck from the Universe. The luckiness of the number seven also dates back to ancient times. Although often misinterpreted due to superstitions, these two numbers are frequently viewed as signs throughout Western history.

> The Universe is like Amazon but so much bigger.
> It's limitless—everything you can imagine and so much more.
> It goes beyond what your imagination is capable of processing.

The Universe is like Amazon but so much bigger. It's limitless—everything you can imagine and so much more. It goes beyond what your imagination is capable of processing. Like Amazon, all you have to do is place the order

---

2   Barbara Maranzani, "What's so Unlucky about the Number 13?," History.com, August 10, 2021, https://www.history.com/news/whats-so-unlucky-about-the-number-13.

and wait for the Universe to deliver. You do not need to know who the delivery person will be or how it will get to you, and you do not get to dictate the exact delivery time. The order has been placed, and it's already yours. You just need to trust that it's on its way to you in due time.

In some ways, it's about letting go of the need to control the outcome and surrender to the flow, to that inner knowing, understanding that everything will work out as it's supposed to. I always say, "Everything works out for the best," even if it may not immediately appear that way.

In Tune With Yourself

Sometimes, guiding signs come visually as numbers, but your body is one of the best tools you have to receive guidance through your senses and sensations. Have you ever experienced a situation, and despite what your normal reaction would be, you have a sudden, very strong, out-of-nowhere, oh my God, do not go sensation? It could manifest as a voice you almost hear, except it's not like an outside voice speaking to you. It's more like an internal sense where you hear it, but it's in your head, like a passing thought that doesn't go away. As you explored in the previous chapter, that's your intuition. But you might disregard it if you aren't aware.

If you disregard your intuition, you will continue to be disconnected from it. The key to connecting with your intuition is to tune into it. Listen for a voice or feel for the sensation when a sudden need to leave arises. That sensation you feel is the energy that shapes your choices and actions (or inactions). Do you listen to the energetic vibration or disregard your intuition?

Let me give an example of a situation when I was waiting for an Uber. According to my app, my ride was supposed to be pulling up. Suddenly, I felt my entire body react: *Do not go*, and immediately thought, *Oh no!*

If I had discounted the energy of the situation, disregarded my intuition, and listened to my mind, my thoughts would have frozen me. *What's happening, girl? Why are you acting crazy? Just get into the Uber.* That's logic suppressing your intuition. You might start to argue with it, trying to justify your thoughts and create excuses and reasons not to listen to your gut feelings. Instead, I immediately listened when I got that feeling because I didn't want to find out what the what-if could be.

This is where trust comes in. The more you connect to and trust that feeling, that energy, the more it will show up. It becomes your best friend. The more experience you have with trusting your intuition, the more you can rely on it. Stop trying to justify it. Stop trying to be overly logical. Instead, simply ask, *How do I feel? Does it make me feel good or bad? Does it make me feel expanded, or does it make me feel constricted?* It's important to listen to your intuition speaking through your body.

There are other ways your body gives you signs from the Universe. Before major shifts in your life happen, you can often "feel" them coming. You can be plagued with anxiety, stress, emotional outbursts, or bouts of sleeplessness before an unexpected change happens. Additionally, you may lose interest in hobbies, careers, relationships, or goals.

It's critical to listen and respect your body when this happens. Do not avoid the sensations and feelings. Remember: Just because you feel these things doesn't mean the Universe is sending something terrible. Change is inevitable, but the Universe does its best to prepare you for what's to come.

The Universe Speaks, We Just Need To Listen

Signs do not always indicate warnings to avoid a bad situation; they could just as easily be connected to positive experiences and receiving guidance from above. Years ago, I visited my cousins who had lost their mom when they were young, which left a void that never quite eased. I wanted to be there for them, to give them some emotional support I could tell they desperately needed. When I arrived, they were so emotionally closed off. I felt this urge inside me to tell them that if they ever missed their mom and wished for her advice, they could watch out for a sign, like a butterfly or a rainbow. Both my cousins just stared at me, and finally, one of them shared that a butterfly had been appearing near her window almost every morning for years since their mom passed away. I got chills. How amazing! Now they know their mom is near them.

There are so many ways that the Universe communicates with us. I frequently receive signs through songs on the radio. (This one never ceases to amaze me.) Sometimes, songs come on the radio that I have never heard before, just when I think of something. When I think of someone who has passed on, I often see a butterfly fly next to me, and frequently, it's a white one. And sometimes, when I'm at a loss and need guidance, I see a rainbow, and then I know everything will be okay.

When you align your inner world with your desired outer world, your energy shifts. You begin to feel a sense of inner freedom and can release the shackles of the limiting beliefs and past conditioning that's hacked you. Remember: You are not just a body that goes through life affected by your experiences. There are signs and patterns guiding you.

Pay attention to your energetic state. Is it preventing you from seeing the signs the Universe is sending you? Whether through numbers, butterflies, rainbows, songs on the radio, dreams, bodily sensations, or anything else you are attuned to, the more you connect with the side of yourself that recognizes those synchronicities, the faster and easier you start to receive signs. You need to align your energy, respect the signs, and allow and accept them in order to bring more of them into your life, which, in turn, helps your life flow with more ease and harmony.

The Universe has a funny sense of humor. You just have to be open to receiving the signs, and you will start to receive guided messages. Do not miss out on all it has to say!

The unexamined life is not worth living.

Socrates

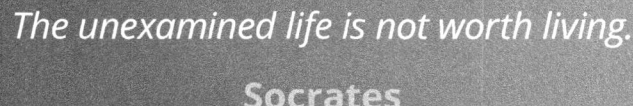

CHAPTER FOUR

Unconscious Contracts

To make the best decisions in life, you need to trust your intuition and perception. Your perception is based on your beliefs, which comprise the stories about your life. I do not mean the stories others tell about you (although that plays a part); I mean the stories you tell yourself. These stories are the first part of the STEER Method™. The meaning you assign to them will shape your thoughts, affect your emotions and energy, and produce a result. So, what are your thoughts, emotions, energy, and results of these stories? Where do the stories come from?

Think about all the contracts you've signed in your life. Would you ever buy a house or accept a job without reading the contract? I hope not. You read the fine print and understand what you are agreeing to. But what about the contracts you have with yourself? Chances are, you have unconsciously accepted certain contracts as your truth without reading the fine print. These unexamined contracts perpetuate the stories that have hacked who you are and can be the root cause of limiting beliefs and behaviors.

But do not worry; the power to change these contracts lies within you. This is another hack you can unhack yourself from. Let us examine these contracts and shred the ones that no longer fit your desired life.

The Hidden Agreements That Bind You

Stories constantly replay in your mind and direct you on what unconscious contracts you "sign." Like my client manifesting a soulmate, the unconscious agreements you make from an unhealed, hacked state of mind can have unintended consequences. For example, many of my high-profile clients—professionals, financial executives, etc.—have an unconscious agreement

(a subconscious truth) and stories they perpetuate in themselves that say they must work extra-long hours, nights, and weekends. The consequences of this can be health issues, loss of relationships, and even loss of their identity if they lose the job that fulfills their unconscious agreement.

How many moms have tried to achieve being a "good mom?" Their fear of being labeled "bad" causes them to create unconscious stories that tell them to follow popular advice on parenting from their peers or examples of their own upbringing. They can often be so overly critical of their "performance" as a mother that they completely discount their instincts, perpetuating the "hacked cycle" with their children.

Sadly, everyone has a version of this.

- *Love*
- *Career*
- *Self-love*
- *Finances*
- *Friendships*

What contracts have you unconsciously accepted as your truth? Sometimes, you create these conditions, rules, and demands because it'll keep you blocked. It stems from the fear that being seen, felt, and loved for who you are is too much to bear. And so you might find yourself judging harshly, rejecting too fast, or not giving chances so you can keep running away. But in the end, you are just running away from yourself. Notice how the story you tell yourself not only protects you but imprisons and limits you, too.

Your life is full of these unexamined contracts. It's time to change your rules, rewrite your contracts, and reframe your story and thoughts. Do not forget that you are a powerful creator of your life experiences and can write new stories and sign different, conscious contracts.

Revealing Unconscious Contracts

Now that you are aware of what unconscious contracts are, how do you uncover yours? Start by reviewing your current circumstances and environment. Look closely at the rules and beliefs—the story you tell yourself—that guide your actions and decisions. Do these rules align with your desired life and aspirations? If not, it's time to shred those contracts that are no longer serving you and write new ones that align with your true desires.

For example, instead of feeling like you have to work longer hours, you can create a new contract that says, "The number of hours I work doesn't define my worth or make me a better employee. I deserve compensation for the tremendous value that I bring." This new contract can empower you to set boundaries and prioritize self-care.

Maybe you struggle with finding love because you believe you must be the perfect partner 24/7, even if that means sacrificing your happiness. Instead, write a new contract: *I am enough just as I am and deserve to be loved and accepted for who I am. I am worthy of love and can find it while staying true to my authentic self.* This new contract creates a new story in your mind that can free you from the pressure to be someone and allow you to live authentically and connect more deeply with others.

It's important to ask yourself, "Who would I need to be in order to live by these contracts?" Sometimes, your contracts can create conflicting desires and prevent you from achieving what you truly want. Do not let your contracts create stories that hold you back from living the life you desire.

The beliefs I held about what being a healer meant kept me from stepping into this role. I told myself that being a healer meant being weird and potentially being rejected by my family and friends. On top of that, there was a long-standing belief that you can't make a living doing that kind of work. Instead, I rewrote the story, which changed my beliefs: *I can be a healer, have fun, be true to myself, and be successful while serving others and living my purpose.* I embraced listening to my intuition, trusting my inner guidance and redefining perceptions and expectations about being a healer.

Remember, you have the power to rewrite your own rules to live by and change the beliefs and behaviors that no longer serve you. So, my friend, take some time to examine your unconscious contracts and rewrite them to serve you better. You can live a more fulfilling and authentic life when you break free from these self-imposed limitations.

Now, let us look deeper into your unconscious contracts and the unintended benefits they bring you.

Unintended Consequences

Sometimes, unconscious contracts create unintended perks as well as unintentional repercussions. Let me break it down. Say you've got this unwritten deal going on in your mind — you feel like you deserve some time off, want to be left alone, crave some me time, or do not want to do something required of you. Seems harmless, right? But here's the twist: this unconscious agreement can manifest in unintended consequences of becoming ill or experiencing pain. For instance, a person who subconsciously believes they deserve time off, but is too afraid to ask, may find themselves frequently getting sick as a justified reason to stay home.

Specifically, about pain, it serves you by affirming your unconscious contracts and stories, the unwritten agreements and convictions that shape your life and impact your perceptions of the world. For example, someone who believes success requires working long hours may experience physical and emotional stress, which can manifest as pain. This creates a loop of unconscious thoughts stemming from that story with unintentional consequences: pain confirms their belief, strengthening their resolve to pursue their goals, which creates more stress and returns them to confirmation through pain.

Despite pain being a significant unintended consequence, it's important to note that pain is not always as negative as it is made out to be. While you often view it as something to be feared or quickly remedied, it's important to understand that pain has a divine purpose in your life, even if it doesn't initially seem so. Pain serves you by presenting you with unconscious gifts and blessings. You receive these rewards through your pain, even if you do not immediately see them. For instance, someone who struggles with chronic pain may receive a surge of love, compassion, and support from those around them. They may also be given the opportunity to step away from their daily obligations, giving their mind, body, and spirit much-needed rest and rejuvenation.

When it comes to pain, it is there to make you see those hidden agreements and stories that are quietly running the show behind the scenes. Pain serves as a messenger, affirming your unconscious contracts and stories—the unspoken rules that mold your life and influence how you perceive the world. So, when pain shows up, it is a signal calling for your attention—a clear indication not to be ignored. It points to something important happening beneath the surface. (Pain is discussed more in Chapter Ten.)

While unintended benefits and self-imposed narratives may occasionally result in adverse consequences, like physical discomfort and emotional turmoil, they also serve as catalysts for growth and transformation. By becoming aware of these unconscious agreements and beliefs, you can choose to re-evaluate and redefine what success, happiness, and well-being mean to you. This leads to a life that is more fulfilling, balanced, and free from unnecessary pain.

Let us review these agreements and discard the ones that no longer align with your envisioned life.

Rewrite Your Story

How does one become a butterfly?
You have to want to learn to fly
so much that you are willing to
give up being a caterpillar.

Trina Paulus, *Hope For The Flowers*

Once you have discarded the unconscious contracts that no longer align with the life you aspire to live, the STEER Method™ can help you change your story by purposefully rewriting your story. It's time to move from the caterpillar's limited perspective to the boundless and unrestricted butterfly version of you. It's about unlearning and discarding the past beliefs and thoughts that no longer serve you. Here are two steps from The STEER Method™ to help you rewrite your story.

1. Identify the common negative phrases you repeat yourself throughout the day. For example, "I never have enough time or money. You may not notice immediately, but gradually, you start believing all these negative phrases and thoughts. This leads to you attracting negative conditions that will serve as a confirmation of those thoughts and beliefs.

2. Rewrite those thoughts and replace phrases like "I am sick," "I am anxious," and "I am tired," with "I feel" because it's not who you are but how you feel. Saying "This is who I am" and This is how I am" causes you to attach to that story and the belief that you are a certain way that's not changeable, creating an entire identity based on that belief. Instead, start noticing these thoughts and recognize that it's not who you are but what you experience at any given moment. You can further reprogram your mind for more joy and success. For example, instead of saying, "I never have the right opportunities," you can replace it with "I always have amazing opportunities" or "Amazing opportunities are waiting for me and somehow always find me." How does this feel in comparison to the previous version?

Finally, remember this: "Every day, in every way, I'm getting better and better."[3] Write down this mantra somewhere you frequently look so you can repeat it when your past beliefs and unconscious contracts try to interrupt your evolving story.

When you acknowledge your unconditional contracts, discover their source and benefits/consequences, and work toward healing those generational contracts, you take major steps toward living an extraordinary life.

There's still a road to travel to get there, which can sometimes feel long, dark, and quite emotional, but each step you take will lead you closer to a life of abundance and fulfillment. You are not alone on this journey. I'm walking with you, illuminating your path and showing you the shortcuts to rewrite your story. Now, let us focus on those emotions and how they affect your story.

3   Émile Coué, *Self Mastery Through Conscious Autosuggestion* (United States, 2019)

Healing takes courage, and we all have courage, even if we have to dig a little to find it.

Tori Amos

CHAPTER FIVE

Emotions

Humans are emotional beings and feel a range of emotions, including anger, happiness, sadness, and fear. While we have often been taught to suppress emotions, we know today that emotions serve a purpose. They guide you and help you navigate through your life experiences. The first "E" in The STEER Method™ focuses on the breadth of your emotions and how they influence the results you experience. It is your thoughts that trigger your emotions, and in turn, your emotions affect your entire energy field. It is your thoughts that trigger your emotions, and in turn, your emotions affect your entire energy field.

> Those unresolved emotions cause physical sensations
> in your body and can carry painful consequences:
> They can leave you feeling drained and sabotage
> your life in more ways than you can imagine.

When you fall back on archaic societal norms and deny, reject. judge, or suppress your emotions, they get lodged and sometimes buried deeply in the body's cellular memory and subconscious mind, leading to stress, overwhelm, and burnout. Those unresolved emotions cause physical sensations in your body and can carry painful consequences: They can leave you feeling drained and sabotage your life in more ways than you can imagine. If left unattended, they may eventually lead to physical disease.

Through the journey of healing my own trauma and the years of helping countless clients with this, I have come to realize that unresolved emotions

are like parasites that slowly eat away at you, but you are not fully aware of their presence. They leave you feeling disconnected from yourself and your purpose and pull you into the dramas of everyday life, where you get caught up and lose sight of your true path. On the physical level, they cause constriction in the body, leading to all sorts of pains, muscle contractions, and disease. In other words, unprocessed emotions can mentally, emotionally, and physically hack you. Hopefully, this gives you an idea of how unprocessed emotions can lead you to attract and be drawn to unhealthy situations and partners, keeping you entangled in destructive relationships and wreaking havoc with your physical and emotional health and financial success. I have been there. Trauma can do that to you. And I am sorry if you've had to endure that. But the more you resist feeling and experiencing your emotions, the more it'll hurt.

Here are just some ways that unprocessed emotions wreak havoc:

- *Depression and anxiety*
- *Substance abuse*
- *Chronic Fatigue*
- *Mystery pains*
- *Overreacting or being easily triggered*
- *Inflammation in the body*
- *Unhappy relationships*
- *Unfulfilling career or jobs*
- *Illnesses*

When we uncover and release those unprocessed emotions, it can feel like a heavy weight has been lifted, or like the light has been turned on inside you where it was dark for so long. Once that stuck energy is released, you can choose to think of the experience, but it no longer triggers you. It brings an amazing sense of emotional liberation.

The Emotional Yo-Yo

Releasing stuck emotions is the key to unlocking stuck energy. An important question to ask yourself is why you are allowing the circumstance, which is an outside force, to determine how you will feel emotionally. It's important to distinguish your circumstances and your internal emotional state. You have been programmed to live in a reactive state of "life happens to me, and I respond." This is what I call being an emotional yo-yo. When you live in that yo-yo state, your outside world—people, situations, or anything from weather to traffic on the road—constantly dictates how you feel, so you continuously give away your power. Once you learn to become a conscious observer but *choose* not to get emotionally dragged down, you start to reclaim your power and eventually learn to be in charge of your emotional state. At that stage, you can choose to feel content and happy, even if that's not what would be "expected."

> You are a powerful spiritual being
> walking through this human experience.

You feel powerless, like a victim of your circumstances. But that's not who you are. You are a powerful being, remember? You are a powerful spiritual being walking through this human experience. So own it, and bring back the power to yourself. The circumstance cannot affect how you feel unless you allow it to.

Another issue when you let external circumstances dictate your emotions is that you may find yourself avoiding particular situations to steer clear of certain feelings. It's also not what you do; it's why you do it. It's similar to having social anxiety—you avoid certain places so you do not feel anxious. Another example is when you drink alcohol to forget something or escape from your current reality instead of having an occasional adult beverage because you enjoy it. The avoidance reaction is not emotionally healthy.

Living Proactively, Not Reactively

Walk by the light of your fire and by the torches that you have kindled.

Isaiah 50:11, English Standard Version

The Kabbalah is "a set of esoteric teachings meant to explain the relationship between the unchanging, eternal God and the mortal, finite Universe (God's creation)."[4] According to its teachings, when you react, you move farther away from the light; when you do not react, that's when you connect to the light. Of course, light is the ideal, higher plane of existence.

Humans are instinctively reactive. Think of the flight-or-fight response or responding (positively or negatively) to another's actions. You are genetically coded with these survival instincts. But reactive behavior is innately ego-driven. What would happen if you stepped out of the reactiveness and began acting proactively?

Your state of mind can indicate if you are living proactively or reactively. A quote from Lao Tzu says, "If you are depressed, you are living in the past. If you are anxious, you are living in the future. If you are at peace, you are living in the present."[5] So, how do you shift your thoughts and emotions into proactive living?

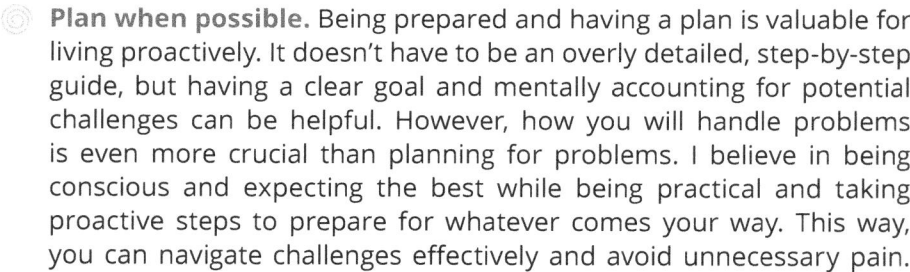

Plan when possible. Being prepared and having a plan is valuable for living proactively. It doesn't have to be an overly detailed, step-by-step guide, but having a clear goal and mentally accounting for potential challenges can be helpful. However, how you will handle problems is even more crucial than planning for problems. I believe in being conscious and expecting the best while being practical and taking proactive steps to prepare for whatever comes your way. This way, you can navigate challenges effectively and avoid unnecessary pain.

---

4 "Kabbalah," Wikipedia, June 29, 2023, https://en.wikipedia.org/wiki/Kabbalah#:~:text=Descending%20spiritual%20worlds,-Main%20articles%3A%20Four&text=Medieval%20Kabbalists%20believed%20that%20all,particular%20roots-%20in%20supernal%20divinity.

5 Stephanie Hara, "Ancient Chinese Wisdom from Lao Tzu: Crown Asia," *The Premium Brand of Vista Land,* December 14, 2021, https://www.crownasia.com.ph/news-and-blogs/lifestyle-blogs/selected/ancient-chinese-wisdom-from-lao-tzu#:~:text=%E2%80%9CKnowing%20others%20is%20intelligence%3B%20knowing,mastering%20yourself%20is%20true%20power.%E2%80%9D.

Imagine you were planning a long road trip. A few hours into driving, you end up with a flat tire, something out of your control. But because you were proactively thinking, you have the number of a roadside service provider who can fix or replace your tire.

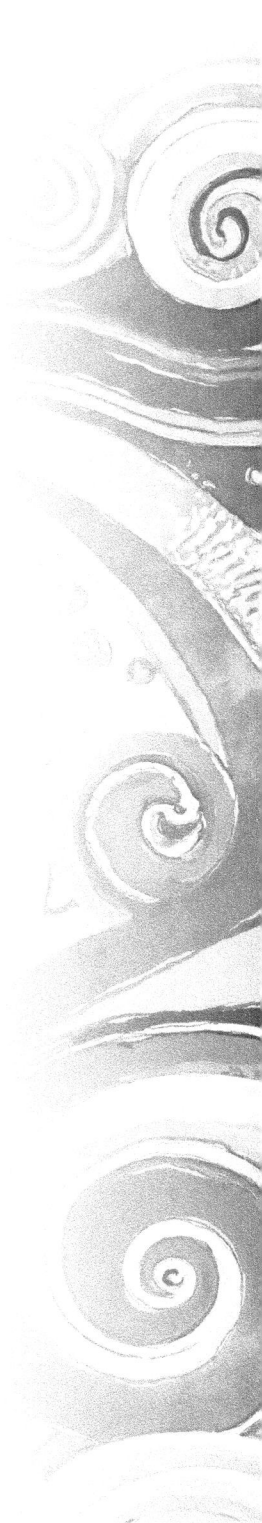

Prepare to adapt. No matter how prepared you feel, something will inevitably occur to throw you off balance. Living proactively doesn't mean you can't react; it is a way of existing that allows you to respond in a predetermined manner. It's easy to get frustrated when your plans do not run smoothly. While proverbial bumps in the road slow or detour your plans, and being adaptable means you can face problems without them affecting your mood. In the above road trip example, if you can adapt to the circumstance, the tire situation won't ruin the rest of your trip.

Accept responsibility. The blame game is a favorite among many, but what does blaming others accomplish? Although you may not be able to control everything in your life, it's important to take responsibility for the things you can. This includes how you react to situations. For example, if a car cuts you off in traffic, instead of getting angry, honking, and driving in that agitated state of mind, take a deep breath, wish them well, and continue to your destination. (This is discussed further in Chapter Eight.)

Practice Mindfulness. Proactive living requires a lot of internal work. This means you need to take time to learn your reactive thinking patterns. Meditation is a great way to connect with your inner self and identify areas where you struggle. Understanding your reactive tendencies and adjusting your thinking beforehand will allow you to approach those areas proactively.

When you heal your emotional response, it's possible to allow the emotion of a situation to come in because it will enable you to exercise the "muscle" of not allowing external circumstances surrounding it to drive how you feel. Instead of emotionally reacting to the situation, you become in control of navigating your feelings. This control gives you the power to create an energetic vibration that aligns with the desired outcome you want to create. That is why I believe the Law of Attraction is really the Law of Vibrational Energy. Healing your emotional response raises your vibration, which allows you to attract things you want.

When you come in from a balanced place of "I'm okay regardless," "I am worthy regardless," or "I am complete as a human being," then you do not let the outcome of a situation affect you or determine who you are and how you feel.

Releasing Attachment to Outcomes

Another reason you might be emotionally stuck is that you are assigning too much importance to an outcome. One of the biggest issues—and a deterrence to any manifestation, too—is that you become overly focused on what you expect the result to be. Often, those with attachments to outcomes do so from a place of needing to be in control and are likened to perfectionists who are future-focused instead of living in the present. People do that because they believe the outcome is vitally important. But is it?

What if you let go of the story and change the belief systems around it? Then you can come from the mindset: "If it happens a certain way or not, I am totally okay." That's it. Whether it's a guy or a job or a suitcase lost in the airport or whatever it is, you can't allow it to affect how you feel. You are still a whole, sovereign, successful person who is strong, powerful, beautiful, and incredible, regardless of anything outside you. And when you come in from that, you attract from that.

It's paramount to remember that just because things aren't going the way you planned doesn't mean they aren't going the way they should.

Emotional Trauma

Life doesn't always go as expected, and as a result of the outcomes, you may experience emotional trauma. What is emotional trauma? It's a term you hear often, but it's not as frequently defined. According to The Jed Foundation, emotional trauma is:

...the result of traumatizing experiences that leave you feeling unsafe or helpless. Some trauma may also cause physical harm, such as a car accident or assault, but you do not have to sustain a physical injury to experience emotional trauma. The emotional impact of trauma can be just as harmful— and sometimes harder to recover from—as physical injuries because it can change the way your brain functions, especially when you've been hurt repeatedly or from a very young age.[6]

Symptoms of emotional trauma include[7]:

Emotional and Psychological Symptoms

- *Shock, denial, or disbelief*
- *Confusion, difficulty concentrating*
- *Anger, irritability, mood swing*
- *Anxiety and fear*
- *Guilt, shame, self-blame*
- *Withdrawing from others.*
- *Feeling sad or hopeless.*
- *Feeling disconnected or numb.*

6   "What Is Emotional Trauma?" The Jed Foundation, May 26, 2023, https://jedfoundation.org/resource/understanding-emotional-trauma/
7   Lawrence Robinson, "Emotional and Psychological Trauma," HelpGuide.org, June 6, 2023, https://www.helpguide.org/articles/ptsd-trauma/coping-with-emotional-and-psychological-trauma.htm

Physical Symptoms

- *Insomnia or nightmares*
- *Fatigue*
- *Being easily startled*
- *Difficulty concentrating*
- *Racing heartbeat*
- *Edginess and agitation*
- *Aches and pains*
- *Muscle tension*

Emotional trauma has unseen yet powerful effects on your life. It influences your behavior, biochemistry, thought patterns, and beliefs. These lead to various undesired outcomes, including health conditions, broken relationships, and financial struggles.

Think about how you react when someone criticizes you. Do you tense up, get quiet, and shut down, suppressing your feelings without fully releasing them? This reaction not only reinforces the emotional trauma but also creates a block in your energy field and holds that constricted energy inside, gradually furthering your physical and emotional imbalance.

Or perhaps you go into self-defense mode without even hearing criticism— which may or may not be helpful. Instead, it immediately brings up all sorts of negative memories and experiences that triggered you similarly and caused you to start verbally attacking the person criticizing you. This reaction is another type of subconscious defense mechanism.

Pay attention and try to notice what triggers cause you to shut down emotionally or attack someone. Here are some questions to ask yourself if you think you are suffering from emotional trauma.

- **Am I laughing or smiling less than I used to?**
- **Am I closing myself off inside, becoming more constricted, or closing my arms more?** (This is a subconscious way of protecting your energy field.)
- **Do I feel expansive, like my whole energy field is getting bigger, wider, and freer around certain people?** (That's the feeling you want to grow and nurture.) Or do I feel drained, as if my energy is being depleted around certain individuals?

Experiencing emotional trauma causes your brain to try to protect you by constantly scanning for danger everywhere. It's understandable to feel frustrated by that, but it is crucial to address it at the root and not

Try to escape the pain through behaviors that try to suppress your emotions, such as drinking alcohol, using drugs, or participating in reckless or harmful activities. Instead, allow yourself to experience the emotions. Cry, yell, hit a pillow to express your feelings and release them from being trapped inside. When you do not release these unresolved emotions, they can get trapped in your body, creating stagnation in the energy flow, which can eventually show up as disease.

Emotional Detox

Did you know that pain in various parts of your body—head, neck, back, etc.—can be due to old, stuck energy that needs to be released? When you start an emotional cleanse, you can get physically detoxed, too.

According to *PsychCentral*, there are three steps to do an emotional detox: Clear, Look Inward, and Emit.[8]

- **Clear.** Just like if you were an artist painting a canvas, you need a clear space to work and create. Exercise and meditation are good activities to clear your headspace. While you are doing this process, notice what things trigger you or cause you to become reactive.

- **Look Inward.** In this step, you focus on self-reflection (a mental process) and self-awareness (a sensory process), building a bridge between the two. You mentally stand up to whatever emotional situation you are working through while allowing yourself to feel the raw emotions.

8 "Emotional Detox: 3 Ways to Cleanse Yourself of Stagnated Emotions," *Psych Central*, June 14, 2018, https://psychcentral. com/blog/emotional-detox-3-ways-to-cleanse-yourself-of-stagnated-emotions#3.

 **Emit.** This process is about transforming your reactivity to the emotions into something new. Think about the "om" sound people make when they're meditating. According to the Hindu American Foundation, "Om is the seed of transcendental sound, and it is through transcendental sound one can transform the mind and the senses."[9] This is taking internal feelings and vocalizing them, releasing them while also experiencing the full depths of the emotion."

Now, it's time to practice your emotional cleanse. Be advised that for the next few days or sometimes weeks, when releasing and correcting energetic imbalances, you may experience the following symptoms, which go away on their own:

Emotional Cleanse

- Yawning unexpectedly, even when you are not feeling tired or sleepy. (This happens often during my clearing sessions)
- Waking up in the middle of the night or having very vivid dreams
- Headache or shifting body ache the same day or the next day after a session
- A sudden need to cry, which seems to have come out of nowhere. In this case, allow yourself to cry it out fully. (I have experienced this numerous times after my own clearing sessions, and it feels so freeing after the stuck energy is fully released)
- A sudden outburst of laughter. This may seem odd, but it also feels unbelievably amazing, like a heavy weight has been lifted off your shoulders
- Becoming more connected to your feelings and emotions
- Becoming more aware of signs, synchronicities, and coincidences in your life
- A sudden urge to declutter your home

---

9   Syama Allard, "5 Things to Know about Om," Hindu American Foundation, February 27, 2023, https://www.hinduamerican.org/blog/5-things-to-know-about-om.

With all these changes happening, it's crucial to practice self-care. Here are some recommendations for going through an energetic/emotional detox:

Energetic/Emotional Detox

- Drink plenty of water to keep well hydrated
- Eat a clean diet with lots of fresh, unprocessed foods to support the body during this energetic shift
- Take a long, warm bath (I love taking Epsom salt baths)
- Spend time in an infrared sauna—another of my favorite self-care practices
- Practice breathing exercises like the 4-6-8 method
- Participate in physical exercise or dancing. This helps to move and release stuck energy, plus it's good for your body

Remember to be kind to yourself through this process. It's not easy, but I am proud of you for taking these healing steps to unhack your life and reshape your story.

Generational Trauma

Doing the hard work now to heal your emotions can help break the cycle and prevent emotional trauma from being passed to the next generation. As you journey through life, you naturally experience challenges and obstacles that can hold you back from living your best life. But have you ever considered that some of these barriers may be rooted in patterns passed down through generations in your family lineage? Generational trauma is multifaceted and can refer to the transmission of psychological, emotional, and behavioral patterns from one generation to the next as a result of trauma experienced by previous generations. It doesn't have to mean some big, horrifying event. Sometimes, trauma can be not feeling loved by a parent or a spouse or having been made fun of or bullied by schoolmates or a teacher. What makes it become a problem down the road is when that experience leads to painful emotions that do not get fully processed. Essentially, they become a trapped energy that is lodged in the body, buried deep inside and seemingly forgotten. Well, the thing is, as Bessel van der Kolk's book points out correctly, "the body keeps the score." When the effects of trauma do not get resolved, the emotional charge from that experience gets trapped in the body and energy field. But what's even more fascinating and often dismissed or not understood is that the unprocessed energy can turn into what we call intergenerational or ancestral trauma that goes beyond the individual who endured it. It is the transference of energy that shows up biologically, socially, mentally, and emotionally from a person to their descendants. If left unhealed, it affects our thought patterns, emotions, and our perception of people and circumstances in our lives. On a more interpersonal level, that unseen trauma generates unconscious patterns that can lead to different health issues, unhealthy or toxic relationships, broken families and inability to create or retain success and abundance.

> If you are interested in learning more about understanding generational trauma and how it may be impacting your life today, my ebook, *Unveiling The Mystery of Generational Trauma*, explains more in detail. I invite you to download a free copy at
>
> ### www.healthandwealthcoach.com

Years of generational trauma were brought to light when I was helping a client struggling with severe emotional pain and physical symptoms that lingered despite undergoing years of conventional therapy and left doctors perplexed. During one of our sessions, I suddenly received a download that was a profound "aha" moment. As strange as it may sound, I shared with her the insight I received that her soul and body were partially separated. Suddenly, she began to cry. She felt my words and, on a soul level, knew that what I said really resonated. Little by little, we started reconnecting the fragmented parts that had become so due to the numerous layers of trauma she endured throughout her life. As we worked together, we uncovered layer upon layer of generational trauma patterns inherited from her ancestors, which had been carried through her mom's and grandma's lives. This process allowed her to break free from the cycle.

You came into this life already encoded with memories that unconsciously hack into and shape your decision-making, choices, and direction of your life. But you can recode them. You are not those memories. They are a part of your ancestral past and history, but you do not have to recreate your future based on your lineage or past experiences. You have to decide to unhack yourself, break that cycle, and rewrite your future. The past served its purpose: It was there as a guiding mechanism for survival.

Rewiring this programming is not a simple process, though. While that programming may have been valid for those old experiences, it has become irrelevant now. Think of it like old software on your phone or computer that's no longer compatible with today's apps. That's the kind of internal software running your current apps: the love app, the abundance app, the health app, the success app, etc.

Your apps are not running optimally because of the outdated command software. I have seen it repeatedly in my work as a spiritual teacher and coach: clients struggling to break free from negative patterns in their relationships, finances, and careers, only to discover that they unconsciously inherited these patterns from their ancestors, manifesting as limiting beliefs and stories that keep them feeling unworthy or undeserving of abundance and success.

Generational trauma may cause you to self-sabotage or attract toxic relationships and situations that perpetuate your pain. Just because you may not be consciously aware of these patterns doesn't mean they do not impact your life. In fact, they can be incredibly powerful, shaping your experiences and keeping you stuck in cycles of suffering.

A long-lasting change can't happen by changing what you do daily—that's a superficial layer. A true change can only happen on an energetic level when you change your frequency at the quantum level. That's why it's so important to be willing to do the inner work of uncovering and clearing these ancestral patterns. By bringing awareness to them and releasing the energetic and emotional blocks that accompany them, you can begin to shift your mindset and emotional state and ultimately attract the abundance and fulfillment you desire.

Through this process, you can also break the cycle of trauma passed down through your family lineage. By committing to your healing and growth, you can ensure that these patterns end with you and do not continue to affect future generations.

I realized the people in my life making me feel small and not enough, leaving me feeling unloved, unwanted, unloveable, and broken, were simply wounded children themselves, carrying many layers of pain and trauma. They were simply unable to be any other way because of their own unhealed inner child.

Once I began to see them in that way, everything shifted. I was no longer emotionally responding to their wounds. I was not triggered by their backlashes or continued unconscious attempts to gaslight. Interestingly, over time, I began to notice that our communication was gradually changing.

Internally, I realized an important lesson: My healed inner child was no longer mirroring their wounded one. And so, their need to feed off that energy was dissipating. This was one of the biggest revelations for me in my journey and personal relationships and a major catalyst in my client work.

My journey of self-discovery has been one of unhacking through shedding the layers of false identities, societal and familial expectations, and the accumulated mental and emotional dirt of my life. The result has been a fascinating process of rediscovering my true self, recognizing my gifts, and stepping into my power. This process has led me to where I am today, and it is such an empowering and gratifying place to be.

I lived for a long time in victimhood, stuck in blame, guilt, and resentment because of how generational trauma hacked my life. But I know there's a better way because I have experienced it myself.

My calling is to help others do the same because I do not want anyone to experience the pain and brokenness I once felt. I lived for a long time in victimhood, stuck in blame, guilt, and resentment because of how generational trauma hacked my life. But I know there's a better way because I have experienced it myself. It's been an awakening, and while some may call it a spiritual awakening, I try not to label it in that way, as labels can create judgments. My method for achieving this transformation has come from recognizing and changing my inner programs.

I have seen firsthand the incredible shift and results that can happen when someone takes ownership of their healing journey and commits to breaking patterns of generational trauma. They begin to see themselves in a new light, recognizing their innate worth and power to create their desired life. So, if you struggle with patterns that seem to hold you back, know there is hope. You have the power to break free from these patterns and create a new, more abundant, and fulfilling reality for yourself and future generations. It all starts with a willingness to do the emotionally charged inner work and a commitment to your healing and growth.

Take Charge of Your Emotional Responses

When you examine your patterns of responding to life, you may realize that, most of the time, you tend to live reactively. You hear, see, or experience something and immediately react or respond to it emotionally. What happens is that you *unconsciously* choose a particular emotion. I say "unconsciously" because it's such a quick, automatic response that you are not consciously aware of it.

What if I said you could *choose* how you want to respond? There are techniques to help you become better at controlling your emotions, stop living in the emotional yo-yo cycle I spoke of earlier, and unhack yourself. That is a much more empowered state of being rather than living in a state of constantly reacting or sometimes overreacting to life. Responsibility equals response-ability, meaning the moment you start to take personal responsibility for how you feel and respond to circumstances is the moment you step out of the victimhood mentality and into an empowered state of being where you are in charge of how you choose to respond to any given person or situation. It becomes a conscious choice. You will no longer be an emotional yo-yo who allows anything and anyone to shift your alignment.

Here are some simple steps to control your emotions:

Control Your Emotions

1. **Practice mindfulness** and become aware of your emotional response
2. **Pause for a moment** before allowing yourself to react. I like to count to ten if something really triggers me.
3. **Explore** if there is a different response that may feel better
4. **Become more intentional** with your words and your thoughts

Empowering yourself by taking control of your emotional responses is the key to shifting your energetic alignment and paving the way for you to be happy and fulfilled.

Mastering Your Beliefs, Emotions, and Reactions

"Life, Liberty, and the pursuit of Happiness" is written into the Declaration of Independence, so it is almost taken for granted that you have a "right" to be happy. Yet so many people can't grasp the feeling. What are some things that keep people stuck, unable to be happy?

- **Trying to control an outcome.** Because you are so uncomfortable with change, you try to figure out ahead of time how to create a desired outcome. But the thing is, you can't always predict the outcome. So, you often remain stuck in the same situation, in the same patterns, in order to avoid the potential discomfort or pain of the unknown rather than taking a chance and trying something new.

- **The need to be right (and looking for subconscious confirmation of it).** Who doesn't want to be right? It's fine to be knowledgeable, but the problem arises when you base your happiness on being right. This is not limited to being a know-it-all. Sometimes, you create unhealthy patterns in your life as a safety net. When something goes wrong, you have a built-in excuse. For example, you blame your inability to receive a job promotion because your boss likes your co-workers better. Instead of excelling at your work and volunteering for projects, you half-heartedly complete your tasks and occasionally arrive late for your shift. Your hard work hasn't gotten you anywhere, right? This thought justifies your actions, but your actions—your choices—are causing your stagnation at work.

In Karol K. Truman's book, *Feelings Buried Alive Never Die*, she quotes Frederick W. Babbel, who says, "Whatever we choose to focus our attention on will automatically multiply in our lives. If our attention is on our troubles or the unjust of the past, they will become our trials of the present also. If instead, our minds are focused on the blessings we have received or the love of God, family, and fellow man, these will grow stronger."[10] You give so much power to your emotions that you do not realize that sometimes you become stuck feeling a certain way, like feeling tired or anxious. You are unaware that you are focusing your attention on that feeling and often keep thinking thoughts like, "OMG, I'm feeling this way. What's wrong with me?"

Emotional Splinters

What you may not realize is that this cycle perpetuates more of the same feelings and thoughts, and it's what's keeping you stuck in that negative loop. It becomes what I call an emotional splinter. The good thing is that emotional wounds can be healed just like physical ones. They just take time and proper care. Imagine you experienced something in your childhood that you did not have the proper tools or support to help you deal with. That is what became that emotional splinter, and over time, you got used to the discomfort caused by it and just moved on, assuming that it was your normal state. Once you become aware of this splinter, it's as though an old wound opened wide, finally allowing it to heal properly.

---

10 Karol K. Truman, *Feelings: Buried Alive Never Die ...* (St. George, UT: Olympus Distributing, 2017).

How Do You Remove The Emotional Splinters?

The way I perceive it is you remove the negative energy, that emotional charge associated with a specific painful event. This creates an energetic shift in your body, bringing it into a harmonious state of alignment. When this emotional splinter is removed, it's as though you are able to focus on the more positive aspects of your life and on your positive traits rather than those you may have perceived as limitations.

Have you ever noticed how often people walk around in a reactive state, shifting their behaviors to the people and circumstances around them? It's like they are constantly being triggered by something or someone, whether it's the traffic on the road, a coworker who said something that sounded critical, a parent or spouse that invoked a reaction, or any other situation, no matter how big or small. It's important to realize that these adults are wounded children who continue to carry their inner pain and project it onto the outside world day after day.

Your beliefs and emotions profoundly affect every aspect of your life, including your health, personal relationships, financial success, and career. When you align your inner world with your desired outer world, you feel a sense of inner freedom, releasing the shackles of limiting beliefs and past conditioning that kept you hostage for too long. Continue on the journey to unhack yourself, and read on to see how you can clear blocks and take the next step to embrace your true self.

*When you truly understand karma, then you realize
you are responsible for everything in your life.*

Keanu Reeves

CHAPTER SIX

Karma and You

Taking responsibility for the outcomes in your life may lead you to examine the concept of karma. Like many people, I used to think of karma as a boomerang: What goes out will come back, whether in this lifetime or the next. But what if you create your karma by having certain actions that go against the energetic alignment of your soul?

At one point, I began noticing a direct connection between my thoughts and the energetic shift they would create in my body and my emotions. That's when I started to understand that the traditional beliefs surrounding karma were not in alignment with my inner truth.

It's like the old saying, "You reap what you sow."
That's a simplified way of looking at how karma works.

Karma is not a punishment. So many people have been mistakenly taught that karma is punishment from the Universe for their bad deeds. That's not the case. (Okay, you can breathe that sigh of relief now.) Your thoughts, the words you speak, your beliefs, and your actions all have a cause-and-effect relationship. It's like the old saying, "You reap what you sow." That's a simplified way of looking at how karma works.

Now that you know what karma is not, this is what it is. Karma is neither good nor bad; it just is. You create and manifest it as a form of self-fulfilling punishment or reward. What you put in (living proactively or reactively), you ultimately get back, but in a way where you do it yourself instead

of something that's happening to you by the Universe or God or Spirit. Think of karma as being a soul agreement. You are the creator and co-creator of your reality. Karma is, therefore, the spiritual equivalent of Newton's Law of Motion: "For every action, there is an equal but opposite reaction."

On the soul level, you always know when something is right versus wrong, but on the ego level, you sometimes want something to be right even though some part of you knows that your choice, thought pattern or action is not the best. That creates an incongruence internally where we become misaligned energetically. You create this misalignment between your thought patterns and your energy, creating a gap. So, what if karma is a way of creating self-punishment?

What if your actions disagree with the soul with what it knows to be? When you go against your soul's wishes, a part of you automatically just knows it's wrong, so it assumes some level of punishment is needed. Sometimes, it could be on an unconscious level, like if there is a sense of guilt, you will unconsciously seek and create a degree of punishment. Then, some situation will arise where you will receive that punishment.

If you feel you've "accumulated" too much "negative karma," try asking yourself these questions.

- *Did I offend someone with my words?*
- *Did I offend someone with my actions?*
- *Did I neglect or forget to do something I was supposed to do?*
- *Did I lie or cheat about something?*
- *Did I break a rule or law?*
- *Have I been selfish or neglectful?*

If you answered "Yes" to any of these self-reflective questions, it's up to you to make your karmic amends, which may include forgiveness. (See Chapter Ten for more on forgiveness.) Consider inviting greater karmic goodness into your life instead.

How Karma Pays You Back

Let me begin by saying it's great to give and donate. The key is, though, that it has to come from the heart. If it comes from a place of giving because you want to get something in return or desire to "do good," it doesn't create that "good karma" kind of energy. That type of giving brings constricting energy of debt, which serves the opposite effect. The type of giving with an attached expectation to it creates energetic stuckness. It eventually can contribute to that feeling often described as "being stuck." A true act of giving from the heart brings an energy of openness and expansion. It creates an energetic flow.

You unconsciously judge people based on what they say and how they look or act. It's important to recognize that you judge based on your perception of life, your limitations, and your life experience. But every human being has their own path, outlook on life, and reasons for being or acting as they do, and it may very well be a drastically different experience from yours.

Treat everyone with kindness and compassion. You never know what someone is going through. You have no idea if that person who just honked at you on the road, that rude receptionist at your doctor's office, or an angry cashier who snapped at you at the store may be experiencing some challenging times and is just having a difficult time dealing with it.

When I encounter someone who acted in some nasty way, instead of taking it personally, I try to send them positive vibes and loving thoughts. I can't even tell you how many times I was able to see their energy shift. Imagine if I responded in the same negative manner to their negativity. That would just create a negative cycle of bad karma, attracting more of the same type of energy and situations that would trigger similar feelings.

Using Ho'oponopono is a great way to shift this dynamic. I will share more about this practice later.

Happiness is more about removing the blocks to love and remembering who you are than changing your situation or another person.

Lee L. Jampolsky

CHAPTER SEVEN

Clearing Success and Abundance Blocks

M ost people underestimate their abilities and capacities. You may be too critical of yourself and unconsciously block your success because of your misaligned thoughts and actions.

Undermining your efforts

Self-sabotaging

Perfectionism

People-pleasing

Fear of failing or of succeeding

Fear of sacrificing

Inner resistance

Falling into patterns of overwhelm

Burnout

Lack of self-care and self-love

There are also many unconscious programs that block you from achieving success, trauma as discussed in the previous chapters, being a major culprit. It affects your thoughts and emotions, driving your actions and habits, causing inner resistance, and perpetuating cycles of unfulfilled expectations, feeling unappreciated, or insecure.

I often compare personal transformation and releasing emotional blocks to peeling the layers of an onion. Layer by layer, you get to the real core. Little by little, you peel away the layers of different life experiences that

created your limiting beliefs, fears, wounds, traumas, and past conditioning that are not who you truly are. Eventually, your true spirit can shine through.

The first few layers come off easily, like when peeling an onion. After the "easier" superficial layers have been peeled away, you get deeper into the core. And just like peeling an onion, tears start to pour the more layers you peel away.

Dissolving the layers of emotional onion is a liberating process that deepens your connection with your inner being and others. It transforms your life in a way you couldn't imagine possible because of the distorted perception of the wounded self you've existed in.

As your true self shines through, you start to feel more alive, creative, strong, clear, and passionate about your path. You uncover the deep sense of self-worth that comes from reconnecting with your authentic self, unblocked from self-imposed limitations and old stories that no longer serve you. You become more available to yourself, to others, and to life.

Imagination can get the best of you and generate a list of "worst-case scenarios" that play on repeat in your mind, creating blocks. (You will take a deeper look at imagination in Part Two.) While working on healing emotionally, you will encounter things that bring up these "stuck" feelings. There are several key areas where you typically form these blockages: Money, relationships, self-doubt, and comparison, to name a few. For this book, the focus will be on money blocks, but you can apply the same concepts to the other blocks in your life.

Money Blocks

Before discussing money blocks, let us define what money is. Money is energy. It's a means of exchange for goods or services. Money itself is not good or bad. It's the value that you attribute to it. When you experience a money block, it can prevent you from having the financial success you strive for or dream about. The real problem is that you may have unconscious money blocks you are unaware of.

When you plant a seed of positive thought, do you dig it up by having negative thoughts ten minutes afterwards? This idea relates to everything, but with respect to money blocks, it can be the difference between living abundantly or in scarcity. Important note: Abundance is not something you need to create; it's something you need to tune into and allow yourself to receive.

The rich focus on opportunities, not obstacles. You can be a rich person with no money or a poor person with some money, but those are two very different states of mind and attract or manifest very different life situations accordingly. Rich people respect and value money; they do not just spend it mindlessly, blowing it on anything and everything, even though it may appear that way to the rest of the world. They tend to make sensible decisions and investments that can make them more money and create more abundance.

By having preconceived or negative beliefs about wealth, you unconsciously create a barrier to abundance. Have you ever heard someone say, "Money is just a tool"? Money is neither good nor bad, it's neutral, and it's how you use it. The same can be said about suggesting a knife will change someone from an innocent person to a murderer. A knife is just a tool, and the person behind the tool gets to choose whether they want to save someone's life with it (a surgeon), cook a beautiful meal for someone (a chef), or stab someone (a criminal).

So, how can you bring your money blocks to light? As part of my healing work, I help my clients to become aware of their money blocks by working through the following two-step process, which brings awareness, clarity, and a solution to their financial success.

Revealing Money Blocks

1. Identify your unconscious feelings, thoughts, and beliefs around money
2. Once you uncover and identify those blocks, you can release them and reprogram your subconscious for success.

If you would like useful tips on this topic, please visit

https://www.healthandwealthcoach.com/blog

Remember that if you continue to focus on the lack and limitations in your life, you will continue to create and attract more lack and limitations. If, instead, you focus on the wealth, abundance, and prosperity already present in your life—no matter how small—then you will free yourself from your money blocks and begin to create and attract more wealth, abundance, and prosperity. We go into more detail about this later in the book.

Shifting Your Thoughts and Emotions Around Money

Do you ever feel weighed down by heavy emotions surrounding finances, like guilt, resentment, blame, shame, or unforgiveness? That emotional clutter creates blocks that can feel heavy and overwhelming. Interestingly, I noticed a correlation between physical space clutter and emotions. Every unresolved emotion takes up an energetic space that could be filled with something so much better. Are there things that can be immediately addressed, like an unpaid bill? Avoiding those can cause you to feel fearful, overwhelmed, and stuck in a lack mentality and reinforces your blocks around money.

One important way to shift that energetic vibration and remove your money block is to start organizing your space and paying those bills so there is no negative energy weighing heavily on you. As strange as it may sound, an interesting hack is to start feeling grateful for having those bills to pay. Yes, I said to be thankful for your bills.

I remember hearing this concept many years ago and thinking how counterintuitive it is. But I decided to try it, and guess what? The more I practiced it, the more I was shifting out of the old program of feeling stressed when the bills came and instead focusing on being thankful to have all those things that I need to pay for: the roof over my head, the luxuries of phones, electricity, heat, water, etc. There is so much to be grateful for, do not you agree?

People often take having the money to pay bills for granted and then complain about paying them, thus reinforcing the money blocks. But in reality, if you are receiving those bills, it means you are benefiting from what they are being charged for. So try to expand your consciousness and your perspective and shift your energetic alignment. Apply this to other areas of your life, too. Do not be surprised if your finances and those other areas improve.

Your thoughts influence your emotions. Your emotions influence your decisions. A fearful, anxious mind burdened with blocks makes fear-based decisions. A calm mind makes levelheaded decisions. A cluttered mind feels confused. What mindset are you going to embrace?

Five Ways You May Be Sabotaging Your Wealth and Abundance

One consequence of your money blocks is that you could sabotage your ability to obtain wealth. You might be thinking, "I'm not sabotaging getting wealth. I love money!" As true as that may be, consider this list and how you relate to them. Be honest with yourself so you can break through those abundance blocks once and for all. (I have been guilty of some of these, too.)

1. You feel guilty or even embarrassed about having all the nice things, even though you know you worked hard to be able to have this lifestyle.

2. You only purchase things on sale and love finding bargains. You would never pay a retail price for anything.

3. You keep shopping and buying more and more: another bag, shirt, or a pair of jeans, and it's just never enough. It's like a never-ending void that can't be filled with what I call Shopping Therapy. You get more things but still feel empty and unsatisfied, always looking for the next buy that would seemingly bring you joy.

4. You keep buying things you do not need and are unable to part with any of them. Hoarding provides a strange sense of security.

5. The opposite is that you only shop for the most expensive or flashy things (even though you may not be able to afford them comfortably) so the outside world can see, which makes you feel more worthy or validated.

Take some time to journal your responses to these statements and look for ways to shift your perspective. Do you notice a pattern in the words you are using in your responses?

The Power of Words

Your choice of words, spoken and thought, is often the source of your blocks. It's interesting that "word" is part of "sword." Words can often be used as swords. Do not underestimate the power of words. Scientist and author Dr. Masaru Emoto researched changing water molecules through words and emotions.[11] His work showed the structure of the water molecules varied based on the influences. Positive words created symmetrical crystalline structures when the water was frozen, while disorganized, asymmetrical structures formed when exposed to negative words. Humans are 60 percent water, so the nature of the words you use really does affect others (and yourself).

Additionally, your words are unconscious spells. (There is a reason they call it spelling.) The words you choose to express yourself have the ability to influence your life. The language you use can conjure the future you desire. How often do you say to yourself things like "I can't," "I'm not good enough," "I'll fail," or "It's impossible"? (Audrey Hepburn said, "Nothing is impossible. The word itself says, 'I'm possible.'" Is not that fascinating?) Or perhaps you find yourself saying things like "I'm too old for this" or "I'm not talented enough," stifling your personal growth and potential.

Saying things like that can limit your self-confidence and create blocks and self-doubt, preventing you from taking a step toward what could be an amazing opportunity for you. So, be mindful of the spells you cast with your words, as they can create a world of possibilities or limitations in your existence.

Generally, people live in a scarcity mindset. There's not enough time, money, food, sleep, vitamins, etc.; you are conditioned to these thoughts from the moment you wake up, but repeatedly saying them is what actually gives you that sense of leaving you feeling stressed and overwhelmed and finding yourself in undesirable situations (a job you do not like, unhappy marriage, toxic friendships, etc.). If you really examine this, you'll probably catch yourself lying about these things to yourself, too.

---

11 Masaru Emoto, *The Hidden Messages in Water* (Hillsboro, OR: Beyond Words, 2004).

> You often live the life you do not like, yet say you have
> no time to make the life you want. If you think about it,
> you'll likely realize it's just an excuse.

So, notice when you say things like that and how saying that makes you feel. Then, examine it at that moment and ask yourself if you truly do not have enough time or if it is just something you've been used to repeating on autopilot. What you may actually find is that you suddenly feel less stressed and surprisingly have more time. It's all about what you choose to do with it. You often live the life you do not like, yet say you have no time to make the life you want. If you think about it, you'll likely realize it's just an excuse.

When you express your desires, it's important to choose a positive language that aligns with your deepest aspirations. Instead of focusing on what you do not want or do not have, you should declare what you do want. This positive language creates a vibration of positivity and helps to attract the experiences and outcomes you desire into your life. So, instead of saying, "I do not want to be poor," you can affirm, "I am abundant." By using positive affirmations, you activate your infinite potential and bring your desires into reality.

Always choose your words wisely and watch as your life transforms for the better. In Part Two, you will learn more about how to use the power of your words to positively affect your thoughts.

Exercises for the Mind

Now that you've learned how to heal your emotions and free yourself from blocks, here's an exercise to complete in order to break free from fear.

Break Free from Fear

1. What's the consequence you are afraid of? What will happen?

    a. Divide your list into three buckets: Things I can control, Things I influence, and Things I cannot control (a concept I came across years ago).

    b. Create an action plan for the first two buckets (i.e., What will happen if I lose control of X? How will I react if I lose influence over X situation?).

2. Interrupt your patterns using the five-second rule.[12] This technique closes the gap between thought and action.

    a. Count down from five to one: 5 4 3 2 1.

    b. When you reach one, take action. (e.g., Your alarm goes off, but you'd normally hit snooze. Count from five to one, then get out of bed.)

3. Change all your fear-based and fear-causing "What ifs" into five positive "What ifs." (e.g., "What if it's meant to happen this way?")

Complete this exercise whenever you feel fear creeping into your thoughts. Soon, you'll be able to recognize the purpose of your fear and move forward.

---

12 Mel Robbins, *The 5 Second Rule: The Fastest Way to Change Your Life* (United States of America: Savio Republic, 2017).

By dismantling the mental and emotional blocks that have kept you feeling stuck and unfulfilled, you will start to create a shift in the habits, patterns, and thoughts that were attracting the same negative outcomes. Gradually, you will become a powerful magnet that is finally able to attract the people and circumstances you desire.

Your mind is connected to the powerful laws of the Universe, and these laws govern whether you'll succeed in any area of your life. Because of this, it is vital to know how to make your mind work in your favor.

No amount of schooling can come close to what you can learn from your personal journey of self-healing. Life has been my best teacher by far. Every painful experience, every challenge, and every obstacle has been an opportunity and invitation to grow, learn, and heal some part of myself or my ancestral lineage.

For each of us, I believe, it's an ever-evolving journey of self-discovery, self-acceptance, self-love, forgiveness, and ultimately re-connecting with your true essence, the being that's always there, perfect, whole, and complete.

A caterpillar doesn't just wake up with wings and flies. It's a process of personal evolution.

Trust it. Allow it. Surrender to it.

Shift your whole energy from a constricted, blocked, fearful state to an expansive state of hope and possibilities, and permit yourself to dream bigger. Remember, what you focus on is what you attract more of into your life.

Be patient and compassionate with yourself and others. You are all going through your own journey of metamorphosis.

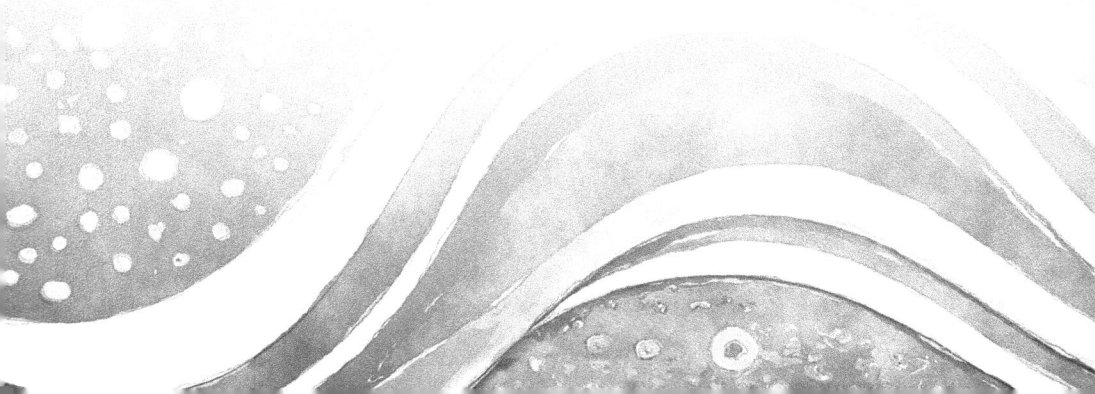

Conclusion

This first part has been about meeting you where you are in your journey. Let's face it: Life can be messy and complicated. If you aren't aware of how the chaos in your life hacks your mind, the story you write and repeat is coming from an unhealed place. This affects your emotions and shifts your energy, causing you to attract more of the same into your life.

So, before you continue to Part Two, complete the following exercise. It is a shortcut for quickly creating an emotional vibration shift.

1. *Find a quiet place to sit or lie away from distractions.*
2. *Close your eyes and open yourself to experience your feelings.*
3. *Describe the emotion you are feeling.*
4. *Notice any sensations going on in your body.*
5. *Describe that sensation. How does it make you feel?*
6. *Try to notice and pinpoint what thought created that emotion.*
7. *Now, rewrite that thought and choose a more empowering one that will achieve your desired outcome.*

Are you ready to discover your limitless possibilities when you unhack those stories and thoughts that have been harming your emotions and shifting your energy to cause you to attract results you do not want? Let's go!

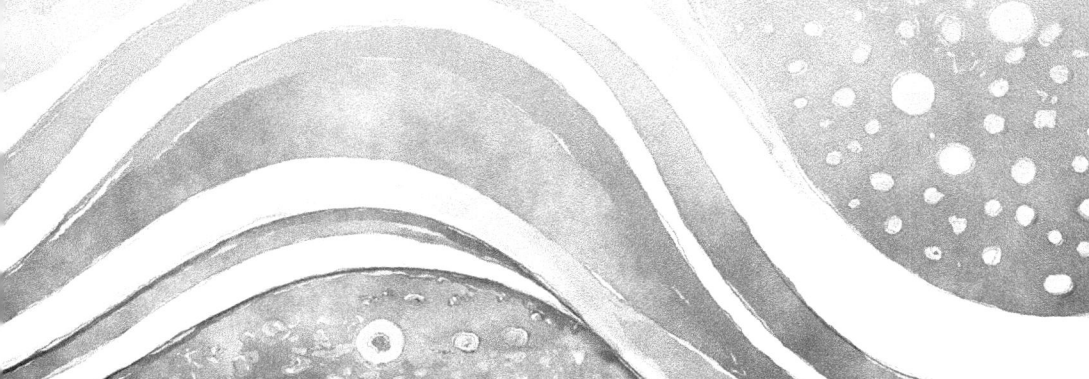

*As long as you accept only those limited thoughts
that have been bred into you, you will never
activate greater portions of your brain to receive
and experience any thought other than what you
have faced every day of your existence.*

Ramtha, *The White Book*

Limitless

O nce you have healed your emotions and cleared blocks, you are on the road to living limitlessly. What makes you think that you have limits, are a powerless victim of your reality, and that life happens to you?

The results of the blocks discussed in The Power of Words section of Chapter Seven that are created by the words you choose often limit your beliefs and can discourage you from trying something new. Perhaps you are stuck in a job you hate, dreading waking up every day to go to work. So many people live feeling miserable and angry, hating and feeling resentment for their jobs, yet feel obligated to wake up and go to that dreadful job every day. It's a sad way to live, and there is definitely a better way.

Maybe you have a talent that you have ignored and are too afraid to do something with it because you've been programmed to believe that you can't make money doing it, there is no demand for it, or any other negative beliefs you've been holding onto—a lot of which aren't even your own. You've acquired them over the years from all the well-wishing naysayers.

Or, possibly, you haven't been able to connect with your purpose. Just because you haven't yet found your passion or calling doesn't mean you do not have it. You just suppressed it with the daily stress. You do not know what you are capable of until you try.

It's time to release everything holding you back, use your imagination, and unleash your potential.

Imagination is more important than knowledge.

Einstein

CHAPTER EIGHT

Reimagine Your Reality

As you learn more about The STEER Method™, you will recognize the strong connection between your Story, Thoughts and Emotions. One feeds the other, so your outcomes will be less than desired if either is misaligned. Your imagination, which is usually derived from your thoughts, is powerful and limitless and directly affects the story you tell yourself. But it's your friend, your ally, and a powerful tool. The only limits you have are the ones that you create yourself. Once you realize this, you can start to change the stories you are telling yourself.

In the book *The White Book*, Ramtha asks, "Who are you?"

You are the great gods of light, the great creators of all life. You are the grand, infinite thought, magnified and lowered into creative matter. You are God, the forever thought, experiencing the form called humanity. You are God manifested as men to continue the expansion of thought into forever... So love what you are immensely, for you are a beautiful thing who has created all things for the joy of it[13]

A thought is just a thought; it's an unmanifested emotion. It doesn't manifest into reality until a feeling is associated with it. So, what emotions are you assigning to your thoughts? Are you feeling possibilities, or have you been hacked to think with a limited imagination?

Erasing limiting beliefs creates a state of mind that becomes like a magnet to opportunities for success, financial abundance, and the right people and situations. Nothing outside yourself prevents you from having success, happiness, and joy. There is no lack of opportunities other than the limiting beliefs in your mind.

---

13 Ramtha, *The White Book* (JZK Publishing, 2018).

To reframe your imagination and thoughts, you need to retrain your mind. But changing the way you think and the stories your imagination narrates can be a challenging process. This chapter illustrates a simple way to retrain your mind, habitual thought patterns, and the story you are telling yourself. One of the first steps is to take responsibility for your life. Are you willing to take ownership of your actions and decisions?

Own Your Choices

Perhaps what we have not comprehended before is that our experiences in life are actually our own state of mind being projected outward.

Karol K. Truman, *Feelings Buried Alive Never Die*

Our brains work almost exactly the same as a computer; the software you use is your beliefs. And just like software on your computer, those beliefs determine how you will act and react to certain occasions. If your brain is hacked by malicious "brain software" (negative beliefs, blame, shame, guilt, among many other mental "viruses"), it won't get you to success, keep you motivated, or make you happy.

Living in that state of blame shifts the responsibility away from yourself, leaving you feeling disempowered and can significantly lower your energy levels and your energetic frequency. To step into alignment, you need to raise your vibration, the energetic frequency you are tuned into. How is this possible when it feels like you are a robot stuck doing the same routine every day?

Most people have felt the frustrations of doing something mundane at some point in life. Instead of accepting that state, ask yourself, "Am I willing to change that?"

The truth is you *can* change it—you *can* experience true abundance doing what you love.

First, you have to take responsibility for what you want and acknowledge that you want it, then take action steps to make it a reality. Just wishing for something, thinking positive thoughts, and repeating positive affirmations is not going to bring a significant change into your life. You do need to take steps in the right direction.

It requires you to take some responsibility for your own life: stop looking for excuses for why things are not working out the way you want and blaming others for the lost opportunities (i.e., parents for not doing enough or doing too much). Discard excuses about being too poor, having a language barrier that prevents you from getting a job or having a career you always wanted, being too fat or thin, or whatever your excuse may be.

When was the last time you blamed someone? It may happen more often than you realize. "My friend is so unreliable." "The dog is always digging up my garden." "Why can't he put his cart away?" These are all examples of blaming, i.e., shifting responsibility away from yourself, from the emotions you feel. In reality, you are giving external forces control over you. There is no possible way for you to live limitlessly if you are emotionally dependent.

Learning to take responsibility is an active way to retrain your mind. It's becoming aware that you are accountable for your thoughts, perceptions, and feelings. Close your eyes for a moment and think about a situation when you put the responsibility or blame on someone else for the discomfort you felt: family, work, finances, etc.

- *How did it feel to pass on the blame?*
- *Did you have negative or positive feelings toward the person you were blaming?*
- *What shifts in your relationship directly resulted?*
- *How did you feel about yourself while doing this?*

The pattern of blame often comes from the inner child's need for external approval and validation, which stems from deep-rooted insecurity, low self-esteem, and a lack of self-love.

Think again about that situation where you blamed someone else.

◎ *What were you lacking when you made your accusations?*

◎ *How much of the blame was a reflection of your insecurities or lack?*

◎ *How do you feel about your actions after this reflection?*

Your past thoughts and thinking patterns have created everything in your life. If you'd like to see any changes, the first step is to change your thoughts to correspond and align with your goals. To do this, as mentioned in Part One, you can start by paying attention to your words and thoughts. If you find that you attach to the low-frequency thoughts of blame, notice those and try to reframe them by trying to see how you can change that situation rather than blaming someone else. Ask yourself why something happened and what you might have contributed to the situation. Shift your perspective, and instead of blaming, take responsibility for your reaction and try to learn from the situation. But most importantly, *you have to own it*. Own your stories, thoughts, emotions, energy, and results.

> Shift your perspective, and instead of blaming, take responsibility
> for your reaction and try to learn from the situation.

The Magic of Gratitude

Gratitude serves as a shortcut to happiness. The more things you feel grateful for, the more of those you will continue to attract. You may begin to notice subtle positive shifts as if life effortlessly aligns in your favor, and more things suddenly just seem to go your way. You may experience more synchronicities and a deeper sense of calm and joy.

Feeling grateful for what's going right in your life at that moment is a beneficial practice for retraining your mind. The tricky part about gratitude is that you are grateful for something that already happened. But what about being thankful for your future? This is where things get interesting.

Imagine feeling grateful for something that has not yet occurred. Visualization is a great tool to create a desired outcome in your mind. So what happens if you feel thankful for something you really want but do not already have? You begin to create it in your mind and feel the excitement of already having it. Then you experience that feeling of gratitude as though you are actually there, in the future, enjoying it.

Guess what happens on the energetic level as you have that experience? You shift your vibration and become aligned with that desire. Your entire being begins to feel comfortable with the idea of having it, and your energetic container expands its size and belief system around your ability and worthiness of receiving abundance.

The hidden power of gratitude lies in the fact that the more you can connect to that feeling of gratitude towards the life you envision for yourself in the future, the more you project it into the quantum field of infinite possibilities. It becomes a very realistic scenario that you are already being thankful for. The Universe responds to that calling as if it's already done. This is precisely why it's vital to be in that vibration of gratitude and in alignment with that as much as possible.

Mental Makeover

It isn't what you have, or who you are,
or where you are, or what you are doing
that makes you happy or unhappy.
It is what you think about.

Dale Carnegie

After retraining your mind to take responsibility and express gratitude, the work is not over. Another reason things may not be manifesting the way you want them to is that you might be too attached to the outcome. Similar to obsessing over outcomes, you obsess over the results you expected but not in

a natural knowing, surrendered, and accepting kind of way. You put too much value and importance on the outcome and how you will achieve it.

The truth is that that part is not up to you at all; that's entirely up to God or the Universe or the Higher Power. Your limited way of thinking may not even be able to conceive in what way you will be delivered that outcome. When you find yourself stuck in a limited thought pattern, it's time to rewrite those thoughts.

People are usually unsure about what they want in life but are almost always sure what they do not want. There is endless fear, anxiety, and sometimes even resentment because life is not playing out perfectly. It comes down to the differences between "wanting" and "having." (This is similar to Chapter Four's discussion about unconscious contracts.) Saying "I want" is not the same as saying "I have" or "I'm ready to receive." When you say, "I want to have," it implies that you do not already have it, which is always going to keep what you want "just on its way," meaning you'll never actually have it. For example, if you are healthy and wish for health, you are asking to be sick because wishing to get healthy implies you are already sick.

Here are two examples of this type of thinking:

Thought: "I do not want to be late for work!"

The Universe Hears: "I want to be late for work!" and will create traffic jams on the way.

A Better Thought: "I am going to make it right on time. I am always at the right time at the right place."

Thought: "I do not want to get the flu."

The Universe Hears: "I really want to get the flu."

A Better Thought: "I am healthy, and my immune system is strong. All is well."

Some people say that if you know what you do not want, you automatically know what you want, right? False. Thinking about what you want and do not want in life are two very different things.

I caution you to be mindful of what you wish for. For example, have you ever secretly wished you could just not go to work for a few months to stay home with your family and spouse so you could spend extra time with them? I'm sure many people have had this thought. But suddenly, the coronavirus pandemic happened. Boom! Just like that, a conscious wish came true, although I'm sure no one ever wished for that outcome. Nonetheless, the desired result was achieved. The question is, at what cost?

This is a question you should ask before you make wishes. "What is the cost of me receiving this?" The next question should be, "Is the cost worth it?" A good thing to keep in mind when making wishes is the lyrics to "When You Wish Upon a Star," the song by Leigh Harline and Ned Washington from Disney's Pinocchio. "When you wish upon a star, makes no difference who you are, anything your heart desires will come to you." As I often say, "Be careful what you wish for, as it may come true."

If a long-standing thought tells you that you can't do something or it can't be done, that particular belief is limiting and should be unlearned. The more the limiting belief becomes ingrained in you, the more negativity it will bring into your life. Note: Negative thoughts attract more negative thoughts. Positive thoughts will attract more positive thoughts. When you notice your mind speaking negatively, simply say, "Thank you for sharing," then move on.

Another example is the "What-if" mentality. Living in a constant "What-if" state can be stressful and unproductive. It's easy to get caught up in worrying about all the things that could go wrong or all the missed opportunities. This mindset can lead to anxiety, fear, and even paralysis, preventing you from taking action to achieve your goals. Someone once told me, "Worrying is focusing on something you do not want." It's true; your energy flows where your attention goes.

On the other hand, shifting your mindset to "Wouldn't it be nice if..." can be a powerful way to reframe your thoughts and emotions. Instead of focusing on the negative, you focus on the positive possibilities. You start

to imagine a better future and begin to visualize what it would be like to achieve your goals.

This approach can help you feel more optimistic and energized, which, in turn, can boost your motivation and confidence. It can also help you to identify new opportunities and creative solutions to problems.

So, instead of thinking, "What if I fail the test?" you could think, "Wouldn't it be nice if I aced the test and felt proud of myself?" This subtle shift in mindset can help you to focus on what you want rather than what you do not want.

(A tip to use: Write a wish list of things you would like to achieve and give yourself a specific time frame. For example, if you are healthy but wish for health, you are asking to be sick because to get healthy means you are sick first. Also, once you get what you want, make sure to remove it from the list.)

It boils down to if you do not feel positive, satisfied, or grateful, trying to have even the best thoughts will not manifest what you want. The key is to have your thoughts and feelings in agreement. Otherwise, there is a discrepancy, a vibrational misalignment, which will always hinder your ability to attract what you want.

My three-step framework or formula to restore your inner joy and a sense of fulfillment and create a state of vibrational alignment:

Restore Inner Joy & Alignment

1. Examine your thoughts
2. Challenge your beliefs
3. Eradicate your emotional blocks

Understanding how your imagination can lead you to a limited or limitless life, you unhack yourself a little more. By taking responsibility for your perspective and reactions and feeling more gratitude in your life, you can rewrite the past thoughts that do not serve you and attract new results. At the end of the day, remember: Do not let your doubts and fears get the better of you. Own the stories you have been subconsciously writing and the thoughts they are creating to attract what you want in life and be mindful of what you wish for.

Are you ready to take the next step on your transformative journey? Let us continue this exciting journey of awakening.

*To realize that you are not your thoughts
is when you begin to awaken spiritually.*

Eckhart Tolle

CHAPTER NINE

Awaken

U ntil you awaken to a different reality than the one you've been programmed to believe, your perception of your life is like a fish swimming in a tiny fish tank, unaware of an entire ocean of infinite potential and possibilities waiting to be experienced.

As you've progressed to this point of the book, is there still a part of you that feels like you have created your limitations and locked yourself up in a proverbial aquarium only to play small, holding yourself hostage to your mind while preventing yourself from reaching your full potential?

I did this for years, living while being stuck in so many stories of "What if". It was as if I was living on autopilot, stuck in some aquarium surrounded by glass walls, looking out, but never knowing what was "out there" or seeing a way out. One day, I finally found my way out. It felt like I had just woken from a dream of self-imposed limitations and the false stories I was programmed to believe.

Suddenly, I felt free: free from the many layers of false Identity I was attaching to and holding the opinions of others over my own to direct my decisions. I was finally free from the many layers of misconstrued interpretations of reality that were passed on from my ancestors but no longer served who I am today.

Any transition serious enough to alter your definition
of self will require not just small adjustments in your way
of living and thinking but a full-on metamorphosis.

Martha Beck

Your identity is comprised of the many beliefs you've attached yourself to. Those beliefs are largely based on the repetitive thought patterns you have replayed over and over until they become an engrained pattern. To break out of that pattern—to awaken—you need to become discerning about who and what you give your power to and what you keep your attention on.

This is why a huge factor in becoming limitless is to allow yourself to awaken.

Joe Vitale described awakening as four stages in his book *At Zero*.[14]

1. **Victimhood mentality.** This first stage is where most people get stuck. A mental filter created by your mind may prevent life-changing information from coming in. Of course, you want to have a happier and healthier life, but complaining indicates being stuck in the victim mentality. Once you realize (and internalize) this, you can begin to understand this is just a state of consciousness and can shift to the next stage.

2. **Empowerment.** The second stage is where you can intend, visualize, and manifest. It's a thrilling stage that gives you a boost of energy. You suddenly set and achieve goals, and you start to feel empowered. When you can form reality in harmony with your thoughts, you are ready for the next stage.

3. **Surrender.** At this stage, you realize you are not God and surrender to a higher power that guides you. Although this may seem restrictive, it's a field of unlimited possibilities. You've overcome feeling like a victim and feel empowered by internally knowing that you are not creating your life on your own. You are now co-creating with the Universe and start to feel like the Universe is rigged in your favor. And let me tell you, this is a great stage to be in. It FEELS GREAT! You realize that you cannot control everything in your life and surrender to a higher power. This stage is related to Ho'oponopono (see below).

---

14   Joe Vitale, *At Zero: The Final Secret to "Zero Limits": The Quest for Miracles through Ho'oponopono* (Hoboken, NJ: John Wiley & Sons, Inc., 2014).

4. **Awakening.** In this final stage, you exist beyond the conscious mind. Your ego merges with the Universe. It feels like the Divine operates through you. While most people do not reach this stage, it is attainable.

All you need to do is plan your actions, not the result. The Universe will deliver the results in due time and in the best, and sometimes very unexpected way possible. You need to let go of trying to control the outcome, surrender to the knowing that what you desire is already on its way to you, and trust the Universe to do its thing.

By dismantling your limiting beliefs, you'll get a glimpse of what's outside the fish bowl and suddenly be able to see things you couldn't see before—new opportunities, abundance, and wisdom. You'll learn to trust your intuition and take responsibility for your life.

You Are Being Upgraded

To truly awaken, you need to periodically take inventory of any outdated programs and beliefs that no longer serve you and clear its stagnant and often negative energy so you can replace it with new programs that are in alignment with your envisioned life.

When you think of upgrading, you may automatically associate it with technology. Consider the apps on your phone: When they get outdated or no longer used, you delete them, clear the space, and add some new ones that will be more beneficial. This is very similar to your emotions and beliefs. As you consider updating the apps on your phone, though, there are often a lot of glitches when you are done, right? But you do it anyway because some of the apps may not work without the updates. Part of your frustrations with this process stems from how different and unfamiliar the apps feel as they're being updated and improved by the developers. Adjusting to the new interface can be annoying or uncomfortable and certainly unfamiliar. It takes time and patience to navigate, but usually, you find that they are actually improved and are more helpful than before.

This is similar to when you experience challenging times in life, those periods of darkness or what some call the "dark night of the soul." This time can feel so dark, scary, and hopeless that you might start believing there is no way out. In reality, your "software" is being improved, and you experience a period of realignment and adjustment in your mind, body, and spirit—you are being upgraded to the next version of yourself. This step in your evolution requires a period of adjustment and figuring out how to navigate the new environment. There is a way to navigate through this transition and be led out of the darkness.

I have felt that hopelessness, fear, angst, and terror many times in my life and couldn't see any possible way out. But at some point, I just gave in—I powered down and surrendered, realizing that I had absolutely no control over any of it. It was not something I needed to push through. Instead, I let the Universe/God/my higher consciousness gradually elevate me out of the darkness. It is fascinating for me to look back at those times and observe that experience.

How long does it take? I honestly have no idea. For me, it may have been months or a year. I am not sure because time at that point almost ceased to exist. It's like I was functioning on autopilot, going through the motions but not really being present in my reality. All I remember is severe pain (I do not mean physical, although there was that aspect, too). The deepest pain was this inner gnawing, a deep sense of void, a darkness that I could feel viscerally but could not explain in words. Many people would describe it as depression or try to assign a medical label to it. But this was so beyond that. I was not depressed; I was being catapulted on a soul level, separated to a degree from my physical being. And that separation was so intense that no human words can describe that.

This type of upgrading happens to everyone. Could you exist as the same person, running on the same software as your eight-year-old self? The updates are necessary for you to continue growing, evolving, and hopefully unhacking yourself. So be patient and compassionate with yourself as you are going through this kind of upgrade.

> Something I want you to be mindful of is that sometimes
> when your energy begins to shift to a higher frequency,
> you get experiences that test you.

Something I want you to be mindful of is that sometimes when your energy begins to shift to a higher frequency, you get experiences that test you. In a way, it is almost like the Universe is testing you—are you really in alignment, or do you still need more lessons? One of the ways we are tested that I noticed when we shift our vibration is that our appliances or cars tend to break down. I learned this lesson in an interesting way. I had a nice dishwasher that was only a few years old, and suddenly, it began to break down every few months. It was getting ridiculous and obviously quite frustrating. Every time the technicians would come, they would find the problem and order the parts, which, sometimes, would take weeks to months to arrive. For a busy working mom used to having the convenience, you can imagine how frustrating it would be to hand wash piles of dirty dishes throughout the day. Then, to make matters worse, it would get fixed, but in a few weeks it would stop working again.

This went on for months, and at some point, my husband said, "Let's just cut our losses and buy a new dishwasher." This was upsetting as we had just bought this one a few years ago, and it was quite expensive. However, as this situation was not resolving itself, we decided to invest in the new dishwasher. Well, imagine our surprise when they delivered a new dishwasher, they pulled out the broken one to be replaced, and guess what we saw?

There was mold behind it! In all those times that the technicians were coming in to fix it, no one had ever fully pulled it out. Now, I saw how the situation was happening in order to protect us from the toxic mold, and the dishwasher kept breaking until we were forced to finally pull it out. And just like that, I was once again shown that the whole frustrating experience was not happening to me but rather for me. Thankfully, I absolutely love my new dishwasher and have learned that as I was expanding, and raising my frequency, everything in my life, including my appliances, were

signs that are important to pay attention to that will test you. They will serve you in their own way, even if you cannot see the benefit of it at the time.

Whether it is a malfunctioning appliance or some other inconvenience, it is sort of like purging undesired toxins out of your body. You go through an uncomfortable and, at times, unpleasant stage when you are recalibrating your energy and leveling up; you are shifting your frequency. That, too, can feel like an energetic purging— making things get worse before they get better.

Your identity is formed from the beliefs you have attached to, many of which stem from repetitive thought patterns that have become deeply ingrained. Breaking free from this pattern and awakening to new possibilities requires you to choose where to invest your energy and attention. This awakening allows you to transcend self-imposed limits. It pays to be persistent even if the benefits aren't immediately apparent.

Similar to purging toxins from the body, disruptions or inconveniences can serve as catalysts for energetic recalibration and growth. Though uncomfortable and sometimes unpleasant, these experiences ultimately help you level up.

What you think you become.
What you feel you attract.
What you imagine you create.

Buddha

CHAPTER TEN

Understanding The Law of Attraction

I f you are unfamiliar with the Law of Attraction, it is a concept that suggests that your thoughts shape the outcomes in your life. As Albert Einstein said, "We can't solve our problems with the same thinking we used when we created them." How you think determines what you get in life. For example, if you believe bad things always happen to you, you'll see a lot of adverse events in your life. Conversely, if your thoughts are positive, more things will seem to "go your way."

But the Law of Attraction is not just another method or technique to get healthy or wealthy or help improve your life. This law works whether you believe it or not. It is similar to the law of gravity in that you may not feel it, but it is there. You might not necessarily understand it, but it still works, whether you are aware of it or not and whether you want it to or not.

Be aware of it, though. It helps you out tremendously and almost gives you an advantage over the others around who live obliviously like zombies, sleepwalking through life, stuck in the daily routines, and never seeing or realizing that they are the ones who have the control and the opportunity to make the desired changes in their lives. The Law of Attraction is there for better or worse, so if you accept it and use it wisely, you can increase and improve everything in your life. If you choose to ignore it, go against it, or just "wing it" by not making any conscious effort about the thoughts and feelings you have and the choices you make, then those choices will be made for you, and it might not always be the best or the most desired ones.

Knowing what you want and concentrating on it is essential for the Law of Attraction to bring the desired outcome. However, it can be tricky to know how to approach this law. You must verbalize what you want to manifest in your life and ensure that you do not phrase your desire in negative terms. What do I mean by that? I mean, you cannot state and concentrate on that which you do not want. Instead, the desired outcome must be specific, and your thoughts and emotions must correspond to the idea of a positive outcome.

Since I was a kid, I often heard this sad, almost resentful comment from my family: "Money always comes to money," meaning those who already have a lot of money tend to get more money—they win the lottery, get big bonuses, etc. Another common phrase is "The rich get richer, and the poor get poorer."

> Most wealthy people focus on abundance and growth and their mindset and feelings about money are positive and grateful.

When I began to study and understand how the Law of Attraction worked, I finally understood that my family's sentiment held true, but not necessarily in that negative way that I was used to hearing. The reason that the rich do tend to get richer while the poor tend to stay poor is because they resonate with different aspects, operate in a different mindset, and are a vibrational match to different outcomes. Most wealthy people focus on abundance and growth and their mindset and feelings about money are positive and grateful. The poor, however, tend to focus on lack and scarcity, and their mentality is often resenting the rich and everything to do with wealth. As you can imagine, those are very different states of being and create opposite results.

I have always believed that no matter what happens, it always happens for the best, and there's more where that came from. The more I considered this, the more proof life gave me. No matter how bad it seemed at the time, every situation brought something positive.

You can change your thoughts and manifest what you want through intention and determination. As similarly discussed in the Imagination section, your thoughts affect your emotions, and your emotions reflect what you think. If you are feeling down for no apparent reason, perhaps it's because you were thinking of something sad. By practicing mindfulness and being in the now, you can become conscious of what you are feeling and, thus, thinking.

Becoming a Manifestation Magnet

Just imagine putting happiness, success, and good outcomes on your mental wish list and having that delivered to you by the universe. However, contrary to how some interpret the Law of Attraction, thoughts do not just become things (thank God, right?). Repeatedly focusing on certain thoughts, coupled with strong emotions, creates a vibrational alignment that attracts outcomes that are on the same frequency. It is critical to understand that your emotions serve a purpose. Emotions are your guides to your consciousness. When you feel a particular emotion, it is a signal to notice what triggers you so you can heal it and release its energy. Experiencing the same emotions over and over and thinking the same thoughts unconsciously creates an energetic signature that becomes the predominant frequency with which you resonate. Simply put, people tune into a specific channel that repeatedly plays the same type of music. Ironically, people often get frustrated about listening to the same (unhappy) music but can't figure out how to change that channel. So, how can you change the channel? Well, that is why you are here, my friend. You would not have found this book if some part of you was not ready to become aware of this and shift your reality.

At times, your words, thoughts, and feelings are not aligned. When they are not, you will continue attracting what is within you and never manifest what you desire. That is why some people have not seen success using affirmations or have given up on manifesting. There is a clear discrepancy in what they think they want and what they project internally. And the Universe only delivers that which is vibrationally aligned. The Universe does not discriminate whether your thoughts are good or bad; there is no labeling.

Think of your thoughts as seeds you are planting and,
like all seeds, need to be planted in soil in order to grow.

Thoughts and feelings create emotions, which end up causing the results in your life. As Karol K. Truman describes in her book, *Feelings Buried Alive Never Die*, the emotion becomes a living vibration that fertilizes the seed/soil (thoughts/feelings). You begin to grow your crop of the facts, which are conditions or circumstances and not alive. It is just like the soil that doesn't care which seeds you plant in it, whether it is weeds, organic herbs, or some genetically modified crop. Think of your thoughts as seeds you are planting and, like all seeds, need to be planted in soil in order to grow. The soil is your feelings and emotions. So when you plant your seeds (thoughts) and constantly water them by repeatedly having the same thoughts while planting them in fertile soil (your feelings) that you carry daily—usually unconsciously—a process of germination takes place just as a seed germinates in the soil. Your thoughts and feelings send a vibration into the Universe; it will deliver to you whatever you have planted.

Fear, doubt, and regret often derail manifestation efforts. They are like an invisible rope that holds you back, which is why many people say the Law of Attraction and affirmations do not work and disregard the concept of conscious manifestation. I am going to try to explain it in a way that hopefully will resonate and make more sense.

As a young mother in my twenties, I was faced with a difficult decision: to pursue a high-paying job in recruiting that required a long commute and many hours away from my child, or to find a way to have a part-time, well-paying position that was close to home. Despite the pressure to take the traditional route, I decided to trust my intuition and follow my own path. At that time I had already begun studying the techniques of manifestation and the law of attraction, and I thought to myself that this would be a great opportunity to test it out in real life.

I set my intention to manifest a job that would allow me to be present in my daughter's life while also providing the financial stability I desired. Despite being told by everyone around me that it was unrealistic to find a recruiting job that was part time, close to home, and paying what I required, I chose to ignore their doubts and trust in my own ability to manifest my dreams. Instead of listening to other people's beliefs which were based on their life experiences, I focused on creating a position in my mind that aligned with my unique needs and goals, even if logically it seemed impossible.

And guess what? I manifested precisely the position I had envisioned: a part-time recruiting job that was just twenty minutes from home and paying exactly what I had asked for. This was a huge life lesson for me and I have since then manifested every job. I proved to myself and others that anything is possible when you believe in yourself as a powerful co-creator of your reality and are willing to take inspired action. I hope my story serves as a powerful reminder to always follow your own path and to never let others define what is possible for you.

Chasing vs. Attracting

Franz Kafka said, "By believing passionately in something that still does not exist, we create it. The nonexistent is whatever we have not sufficiently desired."

If you emit an energy of confidence, you attract what aligns with your confidence. Imagine you go for a job interview with an air of confidence, a self-assured demeanor, a positive mindset, and belief in your abilities. This sends out a powerful energy that everything on your path reflects back what you radiate. You become irresistible, effortlessly attracting your desired outcomes. There is no need

to chase or worry about achieving what you desire. On the other hand, the energy of scarcity and lack creates the need to chase something or someone and is also reflected outward, bringing you outcomes that leave you feeling insecure and not good enough. It works the same whether you chase money, people, relationships, careers, etc. It is all about your energy.

I find it interesting to observe how some really successful people who seemingly have it all sometimes tend to feel a void when it comes to having a meaningful connection with someone. In the finance area of their life, they are energetically aligned with success and exude that confidence. Their entire being broadcasts that confidence into the Universe.

But it does not mean they feel equally confident in all aspects of their life, including their love life. As a matter of fact, that seemingly confident millionaire may be a wounded child inside who feels insecure when it comes to dealing with their love prospects. They may carry so much self-doubt that they energetically repel potential authentic relationships or attract partners who are only interested in the size of their bank account.

The same goes for other things. For instance, you might know a confident guy who gets all the ladies despite having no money. Or you might see a couple who do not look like they are a match. You may perceive one as significantly and noticeably better looking than the other and wonder how this person ended up with that one. Again, the answer is in energy.

To stop chasing what you want and attract it to you, you need to believe deep down that you are worthy of it—whether it be a romantic partner, success, wealth, a dream job, or whatever it is you've been chasing.

Get Off The Hamster Wheel

If you look around, you will see that people are constantly rushing somewhere, forgetting to take a moment to notice their surroundings or even their own breath. On top of that, overthinking, worrying, and analyzing tend to complicate things. What is everyone chasing?

So many people get on a hamster wheel and start running until they no longer realize that they are living inside a hamster wheel...until some wake-up call occurs, like a health issue or a big life change, like a divorce. That wheel encompasses your job, family, outings, and friends. And you just keep running without realizing that you can stop that wheel.

Sometimes, the wheel starts to slow down, and you can suddenly catch a glimpse of light outside the wheel. While it looks lovely out there, you continue running, albeit slower than before. That occasional glimpse outside, the mindful way of living, has shown up, but you have already been so conditioned to live the zombie-like reality of running on the wheel that you do not know how to stop it. In fact, you probably aren't even aware that it's an option. And so, you keep running, chasing a fabled "thing" to achieve. The "thing" you are chasing is essentially running away from you. What you might not realize, though, is that you are repelling it. This constant struggle constricts you and drains your energy.

The more we squeeze, the tighter it gets.

Karol K. Truman, *Feelings Buried Alive Never Die*

Let us look at the reality of chasing.

- **The need to chase** and constantly achieve comes from your ego-based need to feel important, be validated, and counterbalance some deep inner void of feeling that you are not good enough.
- **Chasing results from an energy of lack,** fear of not having enough, and a scarcity mindset. (When you chase to become something bigger and better, are you really ever achieving that?)

In my experience, that need to become something you seek to fill comes from the need to heal some wounded part of yourself. Perhaps it's your inner child that did not receive enough love, attention, or approval. Maybe at some point, your trust was broken at some point, or someone broke your heart. That doesn't have to break you at the core. You do not have to become a "broken" person because of something that left you feeling that way. A "broken" person keeps chasing that high by trying to become something bigger and better, to prove to themselves and the outside world that they are somehow worthy of that love.

But this drive does not fill that void, that deep unmet need. Rather, it is in dismantling all the programming acquired from all the intentional and unintentional teachers, parents, religious leaders, and well-wishers, learning to undo everything you were taught. In the process, you learn to trust yourself and tune into your inner guidance, the wisdom, and love that has always been there, simply waiting to be seen, to reconnect with.

- **Chasing drowns your inspiration and inner guidance.** The result is that you become disconnected from your inner self, your essence, the source directing the wholeness of your experience.

So, how do you find that path that will be fulfilling, too? Consider the possibility of letting go of that need to drive, that desire to be in control, achieve, push through and chase. What if, just for a moment, you allow yourself the opportunity to simply be present and relish everything the present moment has to offer?

Imagine a day when something awakens inside you, and you stop running on the hamster wheel. Just like that, you stop...and just breathe. Suddenly, as the wheel stops, you will realize that the glimpse of light you saw as an occasional peaking ray is a beautiful and bright light calling to you, wanting to surround and envelop you. You suddenly will realize that there is this whole world outside the hamster wheel that you hadn't noticed before. This world is actually filled with endless possibilities and opportunities that you couldn't imagine while running inside the wheel for so many years.

In a nutshell, attracting is:

- *Allowing and inviting*
- *Welcoming and accepting*
- *An energy of openness*
- *Having a desire followed by intention with aligned action and an inner knowing that it's already yours, partnered with a sense of deserving it*

When you align your vibration with your desire, the Universe delivers according to your energy. It is like being a magnet that literally pulls to you what you desire—no need to chase when you can attract.

Here are some ideas to assist in shifting your energy, which are similar to the self-care practices discussed in Chapter Five.

Shift Your Energy

- **Connect to a Feeling of Love.** Getting in touch with love—self-love, romantic love, love towards your pet, love of nature, etc.—will not only make you feel better, but it will extend the shifting energy outwards.

- **Dance.** Dancing is a simple and powerful way to shift your energy. It combines breathing, moving (exercising), and often music. You do not have to be a professional dancer or go to a nightclub to do this. Find a safe space in your home, put on some uplifting music, and move your body. Allow yourself to get lost in the music or the sensation of your body moving. Even if you only dance for one song, those three minutes have done wonders for your energetic frequency, not to mention it likely lifted your mood (emotions). What is even better is that movement helps to process any stuck energy out of your body. During my client sessions, I often ask them to move their arms and legs to help release the emotions we've cleared.

- **Eat High-Vibrational Foods.** Eat plenty of live foods, vegetables, and fruits. Not only is this good for your body, but it also creates a healthy energy shift.

- **Express Gratitude.** As mentioned in Chapter Eight, expressing gratitude helps realign your energetic vibration. I recommend you start by finding five things you are grateful for and repeat this daily.

◎ **Laugh.** You've probably heard the saying, "Laughter is the best medicine." Well, when it comes to shifting your energy to attract more of what you want, nothing could be truer. Like dancing and exercise, laughing improves your breathing, stimulates your body, and increases your brain's production of endorphins, not to mention improves your mood.[15]

◎ **Shift Your Focus.** When you shift your focus to the positive rather than the negative experiences in your daily life, even the tiniest things can help transform your vibration.

There are many other ways to shift your energy so you attract more and chase less. Regardless of the method you choose, you will see more of the things you want in your life.

Your Reality is a Vibrational Match to Your Identity

Sometimes, as we evolve, elevate, and expand our consciousness, we get tested. Now, this is where things get really interesting. It is almost like we're given an opportunity to decide what we will choose to focus on. The important thing to realize is that at that moment, we can remain conscious and present, or if we are unconscious and reactive, it will lead to two completely different outcomes. Allow me to share with you one of the times in my life when I saw it play out in the most fascinating way possible.

My daughter and I went on a girls' trip to the South of France to celebrate her college graduation. We had the best time, and the day we were supposed to fly home, this lesson was given to me.

---

15   "Stress Relief from Laughter? It's No Joke," Mayo Clinic, September 22, 2023, https://www.mayoclinic.org/healthy-lifestyle/stress-management/in-depth/stress-relief-art-20044456#:~:text=Laughter%20enhances%20your%20intake%20of,and%20relieve%20your%20stress%20response.

We woke up in the morning, got ready, and caught a taxi to the airport. From the moment we got there, everything seemed off. It was as though we were in some twilight zone. First, we walked in, and everyone we encountered or had to deal with was mean and unhelpful. Things seemed unnecessarily difficult. From the luggage check-in, where they made us take out some clothes because we were told we were two pounds over the weight limit, to a tax clerk, who refused to give me a tax refund for our shopping until I went back out of the airport, to get my luggage and re-enter again, causing me to now run late, to then stand in the long line, where they separated my daughter and me as we were going through customs.

I can't even begin to tell you how odd this whole experience felt, and all of this was still just the beginning of that crazy day. Imagine, when we finally got to our gate, we were told that our flight would be delayed due to some technical malfunction. Now, we were sitting with all the other passengers in a small room with limited water and food supply, waiting it out. About two hours later, someone came out to tell us that our airplane was leaking fuel, and they were waiting for the right mechanic and parts to try to fix the problem. We were all advised to sit back and wait to see whether the problem could be fixed or if we would need to be rescheduled to a different flight. Several hours later, the small space we were all locked in seemed smaller as all the passengers were getting antsy. At this point, all the food at the kiosk was sold out, and we were lucky to have picked up some snacks and water beforehand.

Around 7 PM, we were told that the problem was being worked on and looked promising. I'll be honest; at this point, a part of me was saying it may be better just to have the flight canceled because if the plane started leaking fuel in the middle of the flight, it would be too late. To make a long story short, by about 10 PM, a flight attendant came out to tell us that our flight was officially canceled, and all of us needed to go find a desk to get someone to find a replacement flight and a hotel to spend the night in. Now exhausted and hungry after spending ten hours in the airport, a few hundred of us went off to find this desk to speak to someone to help us out. After two hours in line with disgruntled, angry and frustrated passengers around, we were finally given a voucher for a hotel, and I was able to find another flight to take us home in the morning.

Now there is a reason why I am sharing this story with you as I realized that this was another test. Have you ever seen movies like *Sliding Doors*, where two scenarios take place and the character's life plays out in two different ways? Well, this whole experience kind of felt that way to me. It's as though that entire day was a movie scene that I was shown, and I was at the crossroads to see which way I was going to respond to it. Now, this is the biggest lesson I want you to see in this, and I want you to be honest with yourself and ask yourself how you would have reacted throughout this whole day as all these things were happening one after another. Because we all get an occasional day where everything seems to be going wrong, right?

For me at this stage of my life, I was able to perceive all of it in a very different way than I would have years ago. I remained very present through all of it, catching myself getting upset momentarily and then consciously shifting my thoughts, mood, and reaction. I was able to see it as a movie or a game-noticing each frustrating moment, laughing about it rather than getting infuriated, and staying very aware of my energy. I firmly believe that had I been in the more unconscious, responsive/reactive state, allowing myself to get sucked into the negative aspects of it all, the outcome could have been very different, but here is what happened next. As my daughter and I continued to find the positive in it, like the extra night we got to spend together, having a little adventure, even though it's not one we signed up for, we stayed open and curious as to what the lesson was in it and what good or fun moments were going to come next. Funnily enough, when we got to the hotel, we were told that they wouldn't be able to give us a room because the vouchers that the airline provided to all of us were not valid.

At this point, we were so exhausted, and my back was hurting from carrying the luggage for hours, that we were just laughing at the absurdity of the whole situation, and I intentionally kept putting out the energy of gratitude for not getting a broken airplane for staying safe and for all the positive things around. We decided to sit back and relax, grab some food before their restaurant closed in fifteen minutes and some wine. A few minutes later, the hotel clerk told us that our airline was able to provide the right vouchers, and we could get our room. Finally, we could relax, eat, have some wine, and laugh at how crazy this whole day had been while wondering what tomorrow would bring.

The next morning, we woke up, got ready and went back to the airport. Now, this is where I really felt like it was a scene from the *Sliding Doors* type of movie. It was the same airport but a completely different experience. As we went to check in our luggage, to my surprise, the lady asked if we would like to add some of the bags we were carrying into the suitcase. I looked at her and asked if there was available weight in the luggage, and she gently smiled at me and said, "Yes it's no problem at all; you can add all your stuff." Hmm, that didn't make sense, as yesterday we were told that we were two pounds over, and now I was able to add all of that, and then some, with no problem.

The energy felt so different, and I couldn't shake the feeling of having been tested the entire prior day, which I found fascinating. As we went to our gate, every person we encountered on our path was kind and helpful, and to make matters even more fascinating, the flight we were switched to was going to the airport an hour closer to our home than the original flight. And you would not believe it, but we also got a free upgrade to fly business class! So what could have ended up a really negative experience turned out to be quite fun and with an added bonus. Because our flight was canceled, we were also given free tickets to fly to Europe, which we ended up using for our big family trip that following summer.

The reason I shared this whole story with you was inspired by one of my clients who reached out for help because, as she explained, she could not shake the feeling that everything was just going wrong for her, no matter what she tried. As I asked her to try to remember when or how this pattern started for her, she said there was this one day where everything seemed to have been going wrong from the moment

she woke up. She was late for work and everything from there seemed like an obstacle in her way. It continued throughout the day and then the next day and the next day until she felt defeated and hopeless. That was when I was able to help her see how she was being tested, and her response to all the small negative things continued to drive how she would react. She finally saw what was in front of her and how we energetically influenced the trajectory of her life experiences. We worked through changing the energy of that day to help her out of the loop that she unconsciously created.

You can certainly choose to disregard this experience and shrug it off as some coincidence, or you can choose to become a more conscious observer of your reactions to circumstances and just how much those affect the trajectory of your day after day.

As a conscious observer of your actions and reactions, by now, you learned that, as with karma, you reap what you sow. Whatever it is that you decide to plant in your soil is what will grow. The thoughts you plant and the accompanying emotions are what will grow to create and attract more in your outer world. But there is an interesting catch in this phenomenon: Sometimes you can try to control your thoughts and think more consciously (the thoughts you want to think), yet they are not creating a desired shift in your reality. So why is that?

Your thoughts can be misaligned with your subconscious beliefs and feelings. It is like someone who goes to a botanical garden and wants a beautiful garden at their house, but they continually tell everyone they have a brown thumb. Another example is when someone tries to manifest abundance in their life. They want to have a lot of money and the lavish lifestyle they see others have, but inside, they feel poor, resent the rich, and completely do not see the possibility of themselves ever becoming wealthy.

When I work with my clients, sometimes I have them say they love themselves. Some cringe even at that thought because, deep down, they do not feel that way. This is sad but also beautiful because once they bring it to their level of awareness, they can change that.

Changing the internal story doesn't happen overnight, but I have seen this transformation take place time and time again. It's truly beautiful, empowering, and magical to see when someone really begins to love and appreciate themselves on the soul level.

For those who are more religious-minded, think about it like prayer. Some people believe their prayers are heard and answered, and they've seen that in their lives, whereas others do not even see the point of praying because they feel it never works. So the interesting thing is it's the same phenomenon of your words and thoughts in prayer aligning or not with the belief that your prayers will be answered.

It's about this deep inner knowing that you either have or do not have. Those who just know without a doubt that God will answer their prayer will more likely receive the answer to their prayer. And those who are doubtful, hesitant, or uncertain just pray words, and then they waiver, so it's not likely that their prayers would be answered; they're just words without the proper soil to help them grow vibrationally and become connected with that energy of God or the Universe or Higher Power.

The Universe will always prove you right, whatever it is that you believe. So, you've got to start to notice what you are believing that's creating your reality. Start to question and rewrite that "I am" statement to the one that resonates with the reality you want to create.

- *"I am beautiful."*
- *"I am successful."*
- *"I am worthy."*
- *"I love and approve of myself."*
- *"I attract lovingly the right circumstances and people into my life."*

After you align your beliefs, you need to start *feeling* those beliefs. For example, what if you believe you are going to find your dream job and be successful? That's a good start, but your energy will not shift to attract that reality until you attach a feeling to it. How would it feel to have that dream job?

So, what exactly causes feelings to take place, and how do you really connect with them? Most of your feelings happen subconsciously. As you go through your days, you are probably not aware of all your feelings and prevalent thoughts—most people are out of touch with that part of themselves. Your thoughts tend to be either worrying about something, dwelling on the past or running away into the future, whereas your subconscious is located in the present reality, absorbing everything that is.

When your feelings are aligned with your thoughts and beliefs, you are in harmony and become a conscious creator of all reality. When your thoughts and feelings are conflicting, they create inner turmoil and energetic misalignment. Once you are able to connect your thoughts and feelings, the internal conflict subsides, and manifestation begins. Tune into your inner dialogue and change the channel to hear the music you want to hear rather than the preprogrammed channel that's been unconsciously playing.

Bring awareness to your emotions, which are nothing more than an energetic vibration created in your mind and body at a specific moment in time, caused by the perception created by your thoughts and feelings in that moment.

The key is to become congruent with what you think, desire, and feel while not concentrating on what the current reality is. Instead, align with the desired reality. Scientifically speaking, it's about the left brain and right brain becoming congruent. So, when your thinking and feeling harmonize, only then can the true manifestation of your desire take place in the outer world.

- *How do you see yourself?*
- *What attributes do you assign to yourself?*
- *What beliefs do you hold about yourself and your life?*
- *How do you treat yourself?*

If there are aspects of yourself or your life you are not happy with, you can choose to embody a whole new version of yourself. As you step into that new identity, you'll see your reality transform. So what are you waiting for? Go ahead and give yourself permission to live your best life.

The Wisdom of Pain

Sometimes, your thoughts and feelings are influenced by pain. When you experience pain for too long, it becomes your default, and you no longer remember who you are without it. In dealing with the constant pain management cycle, you forget there is a way of life free of that pain. At some point, you begin to operate from a pain paradigm, which becomes your new "normal." Think about some pains you may be experiencing now. What is their root, and how will you grow because of them?

Why do you only see your wounds as a source of pain? What if you could shift your perception around it and view it as an opportunity to grow, to heal your soul on a much deeper level?

Contrary to what many believe, not all pain is bad; some pain is beneficial. It is not intended to stunt your growth but is a nudge to help move you forward. Experiencing pain in life is inevitable, but suffering is optional. Suffering is a state of mind, an unconscious reaction to pain. If you are more conscious of it, you can shift your perspective and change the pain response. Think of muscle pain after a good workout—it hurts, sometimes so bad that you can't walk, but yet you are not in anguish about it. However, the same pain for no apparent reason may cause us anxiety and fear, and the more we focus on that pain, the more painful it feels. I noticed that I experience pain when I go through what I like to call a spiritual growth spurt. For example, my health issues have pushed me to study holistic modalities, leading me to help others. My anxiety attacks years ago were the hidden blessing that prompted me to learn and become who I am today.

It is fascinating how your mental and emotional states can have a profound impact on your physical health.

In order to conform to family or societal expectations, it is common to suppress your true emotions and create energetic blocks within yourself. When you suppress your emotions and fail to process them fully, you create a blockage of energy. This is akin to undigested food in your body that makes you feel unwell and bloated. Similarly, when you do not process your emotions, they become stuck within you. Often, you will develop symptoms that are seemingly unexplainable by traditional medical practices.

In my practice, I have witnessed numerous cases where physical pain disappeared once the underlying emotional blockages were addressed. Initially, I was skeptical of such claims, but after experiencing them firsthand, I became a firm believer. I was able to heal a two-year-old pain in my sciatic SI joint that had persisted despite multiple visits to doctors, chiropractors, and acupuncturists. It was only after I sat down and conducted my own healing session that I was able to release the guilt that had been lodged in my physical body, stemming from unresolved guilt from fifteen years ago when I had to leave my children at home to go to work. This experience taught me that unresolved emotions can become stuck in your body and manifest as physical pain.

As an intuitive healer, I am able to tap into the energy of my clients and identify the exact moment in time when their emotions became blocked. This technique, which I call Time Travel Healing™, allows me to guide my clients through releasing these emotions and restoring balance to their physical, mental, spiritual, financial, and emotional well-being. While it can be challenging to find the time and motivation to do this work for yourself, I have seen firsthand the transformative power it can have on your overall health and wellbeing.

I have been humbled to see that even doctors who once had doubts about the efficacy of alternative healing methods have been referring patients to me. It's a testament to the growing recognition that emotional and mental health is just as important as physical health and that addressing the underlying causes of symptoms at the root rather than chasing symptoms is paramount.

Many clients who have been in therapy for extended periods without making significant progress have expressed surprise at how quickly we can uncover new insights in just one or two sessions. This is because I work with the unconscious layers of the mind, where things may be deeply suppressed and unknown to the conscious mind. While therapy can be a helpful tool for releasing pent-up emotions, it may not be effective if the root cause of those emotions remains hidden. This is why my approach focuses on accessing and clearing these unconscious blocks on the energetic level, beyond just the conscious mind.

There are so many different ways to release those negative emotions. I teach a variety of tools and techniques in my course and help my private clients during one-on-one sessions for those looking to get to the bottom of it faster and closer towards happiness.

As you try to shift your energetic vibration to align with a different future, it's important to become aware of your default program. All those old emotional wounds bring down your vibration, keeping you misaligned with your desires.

So, how do you realign your state of being to become a manifestation magnet despite the pain? You probably guessed it: by creating a new default program that is a vibrational match to your desired reality. You cannot bypass all the inner shadows and jump into a higher frequency. It is a shift that gradually happens as you heal and evolve. You cannot master your vibration until you master your emotional and mental state. You cannot manifest a different future when you are creating from old patterns and wounds.

Become at peace with pain. It is often just a perceived pain like a discomfort of change or lack of control. When you start to notice the discomfort or pain, do not try to stop it or get involved in it. Instead, just stop, become aware, and notice what you are feeling, and then let it go.

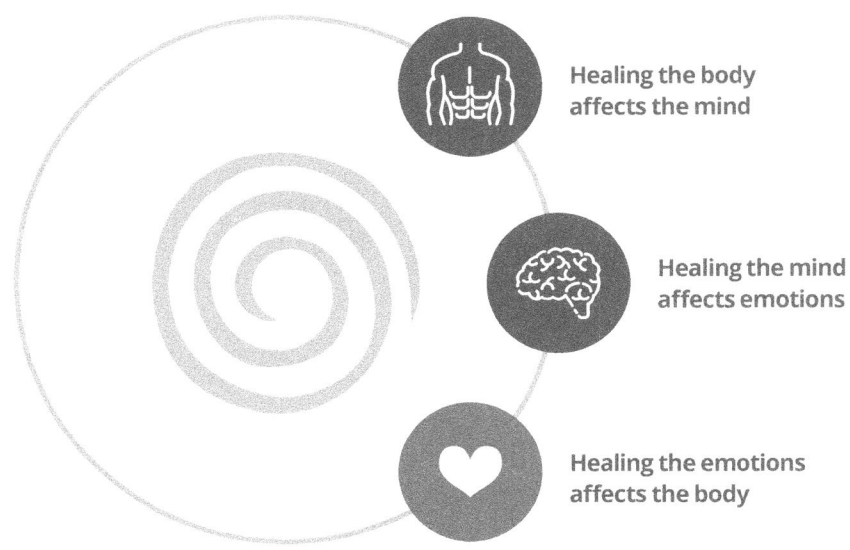

Healing the body
affects the mind

Healing the mind
affects emotions

Healing the emotions
affects the body

Forgive to Live

To err is human; to forgive, divine.

Alexander Pope

Pain manifests in various shapes and forms, and embracing forgiveness can be an important step in loosening its hold on you so that you can be vibrationally aligned and attract what you desire. A huge part of my healing happened in one instant when I experienced deep forgiveness for an apology I knew I was never going to get. It was an apology I had waited, longed, and hoped for for so many years. It filled me with pain, angst, and sorrow. One day, I had an epiphany that came over me like a storm: I was never going to get that apology, and ultimately, I did not need it in order to feel complete. It was not my fault or my responsibility to get the other person to understand or acknowledge it.

I was overcome by emotions—tears poured down my face like a river. And after what seemed like hours (about twenty minutes later), I stood there feeling strange. It was a feeling hard to describe. It was like I felt naked on the inside, as strange as it may sound. It was a newfound emptiness, but not in a feeling empty sort of way. It was more like feeling free of a heavy burden.

A really powerful knowing came over me. I was okay despite the lack of validation and acknowledgment for my pain, that I mattered anyway, and that I no longer had to attach to that pain or to the story that carried that pain within me for so long. I was overcome by this incredible feeling of being liberated from a heavy burden and this profound sense of recognition that I truly did not need any of that validation. The person who caused the pain was living out their own trauma and needed to do their own shadow work and heal their childhood wounds; their healing was not up to me at all. This was what some might call "Radical Forgiveness."

The following day, I felt so free inside, as if my naked soul was experiencing life in a whole new way—without the layers of trauma and the pain associated with it. One day I may write a book on this alone, but I am not ready to go further into it just yet.

For the purpose of this book, I just felt compelled to share my experience of forgiveness in hopes that it helps you get a glimpse of what's possible if you let go of the pain of an experience and allow yourself to set yourself free from the shackles of the past, even if an apology is not in the stars.

The Healing Power of Forgiveness

Forgiveness, I realized, is an essential component in any deep healing journey. When you carry emotional wounds, there is a level of suffering that becomes chronic. It is like you are living in a constant shadow, unable to truly experience sunshine. It is a shadow consisting of many layers and stories of what should or should not have been or how you should or should not have been treated. It's like living in a state of constant resistance to life with your heart closed off

to joy and love in order to seemingly keep you safe or protect you from getting hurt.

But when you live in that level of resistance, you are not truly present. It is as though life passes you by, and you are a victim to wherever it takes you. Living in that chronic state of resistance filled with anger, blame, shame, and holding a grudge is like drinking poison and expecting the other person to die. At the end of the day, the only person you are hurting is yourself. Those types of unprocessed emotions often lead to disease as well as negatively affect emotional and psychological wellbeing.

The alternative is to get uncomfortable and allow yourself to accept that what did happen happened, and you cannot change that fact. Open yourself up to the possibility that it was meant to happen or that there is some deeper lesson in it you might not understand at that moment. It is a process, a journey back to yourself—your pure self—without that trauma, the stories around it, or the need for external validation. It is to allow yourself to be okay with being okay (and uncomfortable), with the possibility of moving forward in spite of the past, and to feel whole, even though you may have lived for a while as if you were broken. So much messaging today is about being okay with *not* being okay. But what about being okay with being okay?

When you experience that level of forgiveness, it is as if you disconnect your emotions from the pain of a particular experience and become an observer of it, recognizing that while you did experience that trauma, you now choose to let go of the emotions associated with it. This is not accomplished by suppressing, hiding, or denying them but by allowing yourself to fully acknowledge and accept those emotions, feel them, and allow them to pass once and for all. This brings you to an interesting crossroads: You can talk about it without the hurt. It feels odd, especially if you've been carrying the hurt for a while because you are at peace with it.

My experience with forgiveness led me to see that so much
of the pain and suffering people endure is self-inflicted.

My experience with forgiveness led me to see that so much of the pain and suffering people endure is self-inflicted. When you can forgive and let go of the past, it is a gift to yourself, a gift of emotional freedom.

By forgiving, you transmute the toxic energy stuck in your mind and body and set yourself free. It is like you neutralize the emotional charge associated with that pain by experiencing radical forgiveness, or perhaps even further, you begin to see some deeper meaning or a life lesson behind it. If you can reach that point, you will experience a leap in personal growth that is often followed by feelings of gratitude for the lessons learned, no matter how painful they were.

But forgiveness is not just something to feel challenged by or compelled towards others. A major part of a healing journey is forgiving yourself. That is where a lot of people get stuck. It is not easy to forgive in general, and as it turns out, forgiving yourself may be even more challenging.

Your story, which protects you, also imprisons you. Forgiveness and gratitude create a paradigm shift and allow you to shift your vibration. Negative emotions, such as blame, guilt, shame, anger, resentment, hatred, etc., or feeling like you weren't loved enough or are worthless or undeserving of love, only create more of the same feelings and toxic thoughts. What is worse is that it attracts more life experiences that continually validate those.

When you view the world through the lens of a wounded child, you energetically attract at the frequency of those toxic emotions and beliefs associated with it. Until you release and consciously replace it with the thoughts and emotions at a new frequency of forgiveness, gratitude, and love, you will continue to relive the pain inside, even though you are not physically present in the past. But your mind and body experience the feelings and the pain as if you are physically back in that painful time. That, in turn, perpetuates a cycle of self-sabotage and feeling worthless and undeserving of love or joy.

If you can choose to forgive and move forward, it means stepping out of your familiar identity as a victim and transitioning into an empowered role of someone responsible for how you feel. This, once again, brings on another layer of discomfort of stepping onto unfamiliar territory.

The good news is that you can break that cycle, and even more importantly, you *deserve* to change that. You owe it to yourself.

You begin to gain a sense of inner power that may be very unfamiliar if you've been trapped in a trauma pattern for a long time. It's not your fault that life threw some painful experiences. That is just a part of the human experience. At some point, it is up to you to consciously take personal responsibility for how you want to live the rest of your life, to either heal and move forward or to continue to attach to the pain and remain stuck in the past.

When you forgive, you release those past hurts and let go of the judgments and stories of your trauma because they do not serve you anymore. You may not forget them, but you just do not feel the need to dwell on them at some point. You may even be able to view them as a triumph that stemmed out of the trauma.

Forgiving yourself and forgiving others means you are:

- No longer constricting your energy but instead allowing it to flow freely

- No longer wasting your precious inner space on hatred, blame, guilt, or resentment; instead, allow the energy of pure love to flow in.

- Relinquishing the unconscious need to stay stuck and play small in order to keep safe

- Releasing the debt energy of "You Owe Me" and moving towards becoming a master of your feelings, your thoughts, and your energy

Sounds freeing, right? So, how do you realign your state of being? You probably guessed it: by creating a new default program that's a vibrational match to your desired reality. One of the best forgiveness tools you can use right away is the Hawaiian practice of Ho'oponopono (pronounced *hoh-oh-pohno-pohno*),

If you are not familiar with it, Ho'oponopono is a short mantra or prayer you recite for reconciliation and forgiveness. It focuses on taking responsibility for everything in your life, including how you act and react.

I'm sorry.
Please forgive me.
Thank you.
I love you.

Let us break this down to understand the parts better.

1. **I'm Sorry.** When you say the first phrase, the obvious question you will ask is, "What am I sorry for? And who am I asking for forgiveness from?" Those answers are yours alone. I enjoy being specific when I recite this, directing my thoughts toward the person or situation as well as toward myself as an apology for clearing away whatever it is in me that is causing me to experience this imbalance in this relationship or situation.

   "I'm sorry for [whatever your transgression is]. Please forgive me. Thank you, God and the Universe, for clearing this negativity (or for erasing the negative self-talk, etc.). I love you, Universe and Divine within."

   A part of you feels guilty or bad about yourself on some level. It is not always tangible, but it's inside you. Maybe you feel bad about your choices or resent something you felt forced to do. Whatever this is for you, this part of the mantra is when you focus on releasing those emotions. Keep in mind, though, that saying sorry means nothing if your actions do not change.

2. **Please Forgive Me.** When you ask for forgiveness, it is an unspoken agreement that you are willing to change. That is why this phrase is so powerful when spoken after "I'm sorry." As mentioned above, I generally address this prayer to the Universe. However, asking for forgiveness is as much to the Universe as it is to myself. It is a healing process that helps remove negativity from your life, which allows you to move forward.

3. **Thank You.** Earlier in this chapter, I spoke about the benefits of having gratitude. When you say "Thank you" to the Universe in this mantra, you are showing appreciation for who you are at that moment and all the changes that occurred along the way. It also is being thankful that the Universe provides you with opportunities to grow, heal, and transcend.

4. **I Love You.** Love is a powerful emotion that blankets you in security, warmth, and positivity. Expressing this to the Universe and yourself accelerates your healing process. Loving yourself in the moment doesn't exclude you from changing and growing. Accepting yourself and what the Universe provides will propel you forward.

Repeat it like a mantra in your head, in any sequence that resonates for you. I like to do it as I am falling asleep. You will notice that I reference this practice a number of times in this book. It truly works for so many things in your life. This powerful practice shifts how you feel and how others respond to you and clears the negativity within yourself that has created that negative experience. Combining forgiveness, gratitude, and love creates a powerful vibrational shift towards alignment, love, peace, harmony, and trust within yourself, a connection to your higher self and the universe. It is time to let go of your old, outdated thoughts and ideas.

Happiness is an Inside Job

It is easy to become so attached to a victim identity that you do not realize it is not *who* you are but *what's* happened to you. Changing one's identity and re-aligning your state of being is no simple task. Subconsciously, it may even seem self-serving. Remaining attached to sadness or anger may provide you with the pity and attention you may crave (consciously or subconsciously) or give you an internal excuse for why you are not successful.

You cannot bypass all the inner shadows and jump into a higher frequency. It is a shift that gradually happens as you heal and evolve. You cannot master your vibration until you master your emotional and mental state. You cannot manifest a different future if you are creating from the old patterns.

While you are conditioned to think that your happiness comes from external sources, happiness is an inside job and can only come from within. When you understand this and can tap into pure internal happiness, then, and only then, can you generate and attract more happiness in your life.

In your quest for a better life, you often focus on manifesting the things you desire, like wealth, success, love, or happiness. You work tirelessly to bring these things into your life, but as discussed, you will often find that even when you attain them, they do not bring you the lasting satisfaction or joy that you seek. The reason for this is simple: You have not yet shifted your focus from what you want to why you want it.

Shift your focus from what you want to why you want it.

To truly align with the vibration of the objects of your desire, you need to understand the underlying reason behind your desire.

- *What is it you are truly seeking?*
- *Is it a status symbol?*
- *Is it something you need in order to feel better about yourself? More worthy? More loved? More successful or accomplished or accepted?*
- *Is it freedom and independence?*

When you allow yourself to be radically honest with yourself and are able to figure out the reason behind the emotional disconnect between your conscious desire and unconscious blocks that are preventing it from becoming realized, you can then align your vibration with that of the object of your desire and avoid the discrepancy of feeling like it is out of your reach.

For example, if you desire wealth, you must ask yourself why you want it. Is it because you believe it will bring you security and stability? Will it make you feel more valuable and worthy? Once you understand the true reason behind your desire for wealth, you can align your vibration with that of abundance and create a greater likelihood of attracting it.

The things you desire are not the source of your happiness and satisfaction; they are simply symbols of what you attribute a certain meaning to, leading to your belief that it will somehow bring you happiness and satisfaction. Therefore, it is crucial to shift your focus from trying to manifest the things you desire to concentrate on why you desire them. This opens you up to a greater understanding of your needs and desires, and that's when you can create a life truly filled with joy, peace, and fulfillment.

Take the time to reflect on the things you desire and to dig deep within to understand the drivers behind your desire. When you align your vibration with that of the object of your desire, you will find that manifestation becomes easier, and your life becomes more abundant in every way.

It is important to take the time to go through this emotional liberation process in order to become aware and eliminate your inner blocks to transform into a manifestation magnet.

There are some helpful tools to help you navigate through those storms and emerge stronger than ever. One of my favorite tools to forgive myself and others is Hoʻoponopono, discussed earlier.

Another tool is this exercise to master your emotional and mental states.

Master Your Emotional and Mental States

1. Observe your emotions and triggers that keep coming up. Those are signs of what needs to be healed and released.

2. Notice how those emotions and triggers feel in your body. Where do you feel a tightening or discomfort when you get triggered?

3. Allow yourself to fully process that as you breathe through that. *Do not try to suppress or ignore the feelings and thoughts that arise.* Instead, notice and welcome them as you watch them play out like a movie until the next screen comes up.

4. Do not judge any feelings, emotions, or thoughts. All are valid. Accept and allow them to simply visit and pass through. The only ones that matter are the ones you choose to focus on or attach to. So, if you do not like a thought or emotion that came up, notice it, thank it for visiting, and let it go. Then do that over and over until you realize that you are in charge of them, not the other way around.

5. Create a new thought that feels good in your body. Repeat it over and over, and notice the sensations in your body. The more you practice this, the easier and more natural it gets.

Not all storms come to disrupt your life. Some come to clear your path. Storms will disrupt your old pattern, that is for sure. And that is when you will be forced to grow.

When you live proactively, you are aware and conscious of your emotions and actions, and that changes the Story and Thoughts you create. You can choose to join the game (at work or with friends) and participate and act in a specific way of your choosing. But do it as a driver, directing it, not just being a passenger—a victim of your circumstance. You make the choice to chase something endlessly or energetically attract it. Here's a hint: Being proactive and attracting what you want is much easier and more rewarding.

So, what state do you want to live in, reactive or proactive?

Complete this short exercise before you continue to the next chapter.

Steps to Creating Your Dreams

1. Understand what you actually want—clarity is power.

2. Understand why you want it without worrying about the "how."

3. Ask yourself why you do not have it. Is the answer true? (The reason you do not have it and never will is that unless you change your habits and thoughts, you'll continue to produce the same results.)

4. What is your strategy to achieve it?

5. What is the specific action you will take five minutes from now that will move you closer to your goal?

After completing this exercise, get ready to move on to how you can awaken your potential.

Abundance is not something we acquire.
It is something we tap into.

Wayne Dyer

CHAPTER ELEVEN

Manifesting Abundance

started recognizing my ability to consciously manifest many years ago and have used this knowledge countless times to attract things I desire. I remember many years ago, I really wanted a pair of boots, but they were too expensive. Sure enough, I ended up getting those boots on a great sale, leaving my friends surprised at how that happened so unexpectedly. That is when I realized that if I had inner knowing, an undeniable certainty that the boots would be mine—even though I didn't know how since I couldn't afford them—they would, as if by magic, go on a crazy sale, and I would be able to buy them without any financial burden.

Eventually, I transformed this technique into a tool, which I call "The Certainty Technique," for anything in my life—the condo, vacations, job opportunities, houses, or anything I could think of. I also incorporated this with my clients. Unsurprisingly, it worked every time for them.

With just a few simple steps, you can start to manifest and attract your desires. Here are some easy examples of how I began to manifest things into my reality:

Manifesting Things Into Reality

1. Start by manifesting coins on the ground and parking spots in crowded malls. Do this for a few days before moving on to the next step.

2. Command your intuition to see a butterfly, an elephant, or a purple car. Again, work on this for three to five days before trying step 3.

3. Using the same technique you used in steps 1 and 2, manifest something you know is unrealistic or almost impossible to see. Watch as the Universe brings it to your awareness. Prepare to be amazed!

Now that you are more versed in becoming a manifestation magnet, let us explore manifesting on a deeper level. Follow this formula to help you consciously manifest your desires:

INTENTION + DECISION + FOCUS + FEELING +
EXPECTATION + CONSISTENT ACTION =
CONSCIOUS MANIFESTATION

- First, set an **intention.** Your vision (intention) will continue to evolve, but the key is to stay connected to it.
- Next, make a **decision** to pursue the vision. This will give you a conscious direction, providing that intention with needed attention.
- **Focus** on it. Nurture it.
- Now, assign a positive **feeling** to your intention and really feel into it.
- Set your **expectations** of the desired outcome without needing to know how it will show up. Anticipate that what you desire is already on its way to you.
- Finally, you have to **take action consistently** to make your vision a reality. Consistency is key. Keep practicing to keep the vision alive.

This produces **conscious manifestation**.

Mastering Manifestation

Before sharing the steps with you, it's important for you to remember: If you are desperate to have something, you will attract from an energy of desperation, lack, and chase. It's important to approach this with a gratitude mindset, as discussed earlier. Now, let us start with the first step:

Creating Alignment

Are you familiar with the Law of As Within, So Without? "It means your inner world is a reflection of your outer world. Your outer world and the things you create into your reality are a mirror of what you believe and have created inside of you."[16] So, if you are experiencing any turmoil in your life, it is always a reflection of some unrest in your mind and a manifestation into the physical world.

But before creating a clear intention, you must remove the static and turmoil in your mind. Manifesting something is not creating something out of nowhere. It is a realization that whatever you seek is already here, present, and waiting for you to just step into, accept, and allow yourself to receive it. It is the acknowledgment that you already have whatever you desire, and all you need to do is tune in to the same frequency as that desire to align with it.

For example, picture yourself trying to tune in to a radio station of 100.3 to listen to some pop music, but instead, your dial is set to 98.7 and all you hear is elevator music. You cannot hear the music from 100.3 until you change that dial from 98.7, right? But it doesn't mean that the music on 100.3 is not there. It just means that you haven't tuned in to the appropriate frequency of that radio station to hear the music you were hoping to hear. Once you realize it, you move the dial and boom! You are listening to pop.

The same thing is experienced in your life through the Law of Attraction. You keep on looking for and desiring one thing while being tuned into an entirely different frequency. One of the ways I see people doing this is by providing constant criticism and angry remarks towards wealthy entrepreneurs or celebrities, judging them for having lots of money and making them seem like villains. If you think about it, it would make sense

---

16 "The Law of as within so Without," *GuideSpeak*, accessed July 1, 2023,
     https://guidespeak.com/chapters/the-law-of-as-within-so-without/

that the frequency of that kind of thought is quite different from the frequency of abundance that those wealthy folks are living in, perhaps one of gratitude for having the abundance in their lives, joy of being able to do more things and being able to help more people. So, for those living in that sense of anger, hatred, or resentment, it is a far vibrational reach from where they want to be.

There are some steps you can take to shift your money frequency.

Shift Your Money Frequency

1. Realize and acknowledge your counterintuitive thoughts and thinking patterns.

2. Start to rewrite that pattern into one more conducive to success and abundance. This can be accomplished by starting to notice the good things done by some of the wealthiest people. Then, begin to feel happy for them, impressed by what they are doing.

3. This is an extremely important step: Learn to experience gratitude for the wealth out there, acknowledging that even though you do not currently have it in your possession, you know that it is already here, waiting for you to align with it, to tune into it.

In Chapter Seven, I touched on shifting your thoughts around paying bills. It is a great practice I started doing many years ago and experienced its magic: I was thankful for every bill I received, including credit card bills, utility bills, mortgage, or rent bills, etc. When you do this, though, it is critical for you to *feel* thankful for those bills. While it may seem like a painful process to feel thankful at first, and there is likely to be some resistance, try starting with one small bill. When you receive it, notice your normal feeling about it. For me, it was something like, "Eh, here is another one. How many bills are there? When do they stop coming? How the heck am I supposed to pay for all of this?"

Let us say the bill you have is a credit card statement. Hold it, look at it, and consciously tell yourself, "Thank you, Visa. I am grateful to receive this bill. It means I paid for the food on the table and the new clothes I'm wearing. I am so grateful to have and be able to afford it. I gratefully pay this bill now and appreciate my ability to do so. Thank you, and I look forward to the next bill I will receive."

Sounds crazy, right? But notice how you felt when you did that. Did it feel better than saying that you hate seeing the bills and resent having to pay for them? Keep doing that with every new bill you receive until you notice that you enjoy receiving and paying your bills. And then, notice if anything changes in your life. The next step is:

Set it and forget it.

What does that really mean? You detach from the need to control the outcome, set your intention, and allow it to come in divine timing. When you have a scarcity or a lack of energy, it causes you to hold onto your expected outcome too tightly. You have to ease your grip so that the Universe can deliver.

Think of it like a restaurant order. You tell your waiter what you want, and you know, without a doubt—trust—that the order will come whenever it's ready. It is unlikely you sit with your utensils in hand, saying, "Is it going to come? Is it coming now? Will it take an hour or a day or a week?" It's unlikely that you do these things. Why? You do not need to stress over it, ponder about it, or try to control it. Instead, you sit back and enjoy the atmosphere, knowing the delicious food is coming.

So, when you've set your intention, treat it like ordering food at a restaurant and trust the Universe will deliver. The final step is:

Surrender.

Once you feel you are in a state of vibrational alignment, surrender any need to control the outcome and how you'll get there. Let go of the need to question how long it might take to receive and stop playing in your head all the different scenarios of where it will come from. The Universe will deliver it at the best time and in the most unexpected way. Your mind cannot begin

to conceive of what is possible in the infinite possibilities of the quantum field. All you need to do is let go, breathe, and trust that it is already here. It is yours to receive. It is yours to receive.

Fear of Change

In order for the manifesting to occur, you have to be ready to receive. What does it mean to be ready to receive? It means you have to energetically align with what you are manifesting, like a cup being the right size to receive the juice that will be poured into it. Your subconscious has to meet your conscious desires. If you truly wished for ten million dollars, you may think you are ready to receive it, but the truth is you have to be ready to accept it.

Your ego will scream out, "Of course I am ready!" But what if deep down, you are scared because thoughts like, "What would I do with that amount of money," "What if someone finds out and wants to hurt me," or "What if I lose it all?" When fear-based thoughts come up, your emotions unconsciously shift from being ones of gratitude, happiness, and joy of having all that money to thoughts of fear and worry. You start to feel unsafe about having that amount of money.

How can your subconscious allow you to feel unsafe? It will do all it can to protect you from getting hurt. So its job in this type of scenario is not to allow the ten million to be realized, to manifest into your reality, because it's unsafe. However, realizing that it's a subconscious reaction and programming from some past learned experiences that are taking place, you can rewrite the thoughts and create new beliefs, which in turn will create new emotions that will be vibrationally aligned with your desire. That is when you can see the magic happen.

When I reflected on my experience while looking for a new house, I realized that during those two years when we were committed to spending our time looking at the houses coming on the market, in the back of my mind, there was also a consistent questioning of why are we looking for another house. *Do we really want or need a bigger house? Wouldn't it be more expensive and more risky? Plus, our house is really not that bad. After all, we've enjoyed it for years and can continue to enjoy it for years to come.*

Suddenly, it dawned on me one day that I'd been spending time looking for and desiring something while at the same time telling myself that I didn't really need it or want it. How did that make any sense? How or why would the Universe deliver something to me that I'm not even sure I really want? I decided to sit down with myself and have a candid conversation in my head, get down to the bottom of it, and try to figure out what I truly wanted. *Did I really want a new house? Why did I want to have a bigger house? How many bedrooms should it have? Why did I need those? How many bathrooms and garages? Did I want a pool?* The questions went on and on.

After realizing that I really wanted to move to a better area and did desire a better home, we continued our search, even though we still heard numerous times from different real estate agents that a home in our price range with all of our requests and requirements didn't exist. But I know manifestation, and I was confident that once I connected my desire with my belief—the inner knowing that the right house for me existed—those external doubts would not affect me.

As I have already mentioned, we did get the house we desired—that I manifested. I hope this example from my life illustrates what it means to align and be ready to receive something you desire, not fear the change of it happening.

One final thought on fear of change. Sometimes, even when change is positive, you can become attached to the status quo and want to stay in your comfort zone. Fear of the unknown and reluctance to leave that zone can lead to subconscious doubts, which, as we've mentioned, will reflect on your ability to manifest. The opposite of this is true, too. If you decide to make changes and become too attached to an outcome, it is like trying to micromanage the Universe, telling it what to do and how to get it done. It can lead to frustration and disappointment when things do not turn out as you expected.

As you can imagine, the Universe has a lot more options and possibilities to offer than you can ever think up. Your job is to know the "what." The Universe will take care of the "how." You just need to sit back, relax, and bask in the internal knowing that the Universe has your back and everything will work out for the best. Now, how does this feel in comparison to the feeling you get from constantly thinking about the limited options available to you that your mind can come up with? Remember, the Universe is rigged in your favor.

The Game of Manifesting and How to Win It

When people speak of abundance and manifesting, they often think about money. But being so busy and focused on making, keeping, earning, and working hard for money, they forget to stop and recognize that money is so much more than the physical exchange of goods and services. Money is also an energetic exchange that carries an energetic vibration.

When you focus on the never-ending *need* for more money, that comes from the place of not having enough, which creates an energetic void, which in turn attracts more lack and void. Not having enough money and struggling financially are just symptoms of an underlying imbalance: in the same way, a headache is a symptom caused or triggered by something usually outside the brain's normal functions. Another analogy I would use is if your car gets a check engine light, that is not the problem but a symptom pointing at a deeper problem.

So, is there a way to break out of that financial rut? It is certainly not by working any harder. Because if working harder would make you rich, then wouldn't all the hard-working laborers of the world be billionaires? So something doesn't add up, right? What I have seen work every single time is that this change can only come from internal change, which begins with changing your money story and shifting your vibration to align with abundance instead of lack.

How do you do that? Pema Chödrön's quote, "You are the sky. Everything else—it's just the weather," explains it perfectly. Think of yourself as the sky; all the emotions, circumstances, and triggers you experience are just the weather. They'll come and go, like gentle rain or a major storm. But if you—as the sky—can remain a conscious observer of that "weather," then you do not attach to what it all means; you do not let it change your identity.

In essence, you can't attach self-worth to your financial circumstances. Do not let other people's opinions, experiences, and financial positions affect your inner state. You. Are. The. Sky. Everything else is just the weather.

> Do not attach self-worth to your
> financial circumstances.

There is no magic pill that you can swallow and get rich. It just doesn't work like that, which is why so many quickly made millionaires, such as lottery winners, end up losing all their money as fast as they won it. Why? Because their energetic alignment was not yet ready to receive all that abundance. Their deep-rooted beliefs about money were not in congruence with the financial experience they stumbled upon unexpectedly.

Why do the rich tend to get richer, and the poor remain poor? Instead of answering this question, allow me to propose an interesting perspective shift. What if you started to ask yourself *how* instead of *why*? Suddenly, that pivots the direction of the thoughts, shifting the focus from a disempowered victim mindset to an empowered one.

Another way to shift your attitude to manifest more abundance is to create a list of "healthy" thoughts around money and wealth. You cannot pour a pound of sugar (abundance) into a one-ounce cup, right? So, in order to be open and receive a lot of abundance, you need to increase the size of your container that can hold all that abundance. How do you do that? You start by inspecting your beliefs around abundance.

Here are the key questions I would recommend starting with.

- Do I believe I can be wealthy?
- How do I feel about the rich people?
- When I see someone a lot wealthier than me, what are my thoughts and feelings about them right away?
- Do I deserve to be really rich?
- Being rich would mean that my life will become

_____ and will have these challenges

_____. (Write the first thing that comes to your mind.)

Having a limited perspective of "What's possible for me" will keep you stuck. Think about how much your mindset keeps you locked behind a self-created shut door in your mind. Guess what? You can unlock and open the door to abundance and success and step into the limitless abundance that's innately yours.

If you would like more ideas on this topic,
I invite you to visit

https://bit.ly/FiveMoneyBlocks

to receive my free "Five Money Blocks
and Bonus Manifesting Techniques."

From Vision to Reality

So, how do you go about creating and manifesting abundance and success? Having come to this country with absolutely nothing other than a suitcase per person in the family and $200 for the entire family to live off of, I speak from personal experience that you can create the life of your dreams, as I have. The only thing standing between your goal and your current reality is your limited thinking.

Here are six key steps to train yourself to think differently when manifesting.

Think Differently When Manifesting

1. **Connect with Your Inner Voice.** You need to tune in and connect to your inner voice. Listen to it, hear it, and accept what it says despite what your ego, conscious mind, or thoughts based on your current reality tell you. You can't ignore that inner voice, what I call your sixth sense or your intuition, and expect it to serve your needs and guide you because, again, you are just wishing for something but not aligning with its energy and the feeling of happiness and gratitude of having it and receiving it, is never going to work.

   Perhaps you grew up always hearing that you are poor and not smart enough to have anything luxurious in life, and that belief has led you to manifest accordingly. If you believe you are not as good as someone else who lives in a mansion, then for obvious reasons, you will not allow yourself to live in that mansion because you will believe you are not worthy of it. Once you start to question yourself about whether or not it's true, you might come to realize that you were just as worthy as that mansion owner, that you are no worse, no dumber, no uglier, and no less fortunate than they are, and that if you desire it, you, too, can have a mansion of your dreams.

   There is, however, a little bit of a catch. In order to see yourself as a successful owner of a gorgeous mansion, you cannot feel inside as a person living in a shack, whatever that feeling means to you. That is why so many people who win the lottery end up being broke shortly after because, in their internal version of themselves, they are not aligned with the vision of being a receiver of millions of dollars. Instead, they still feel like a poor person who has been given a lot of money. But there lies the major difference: Until you teach yourself to feel—not think but feel yourself to be a millionaire—you can never achieve the level of abundance you may be dreaming of because that inner belief and feeling creates that vibrational alignment.

> Until you teach yourself to feel, you can never achieve the level of abundance you may dream of.

2. **Self-Confidence.** Trying to manifest, create, or attract something into your life while resisting receiving it makes no sense. So, where does this resistance come from? I do not know about you, but I certainly grew up being fed a lot of limiting thoughts that eventually became beliefs that I gradually needed to erase and rewrite. Those negative thoughts become your default, habitual way of thinking.

External beliefs can weigh you down, like, "Yeah, right, you are such a dreamer. Do you think that you can somehow break away from the threat of poverty and become a princess? What makes you think that that can happen to you? If it could, it could have happened to any of us, but it has not—not to your parents, not to your grandparents, and not to your parents before them." How do you tune these messages out?

Negativity surrounds and bombards you from every direction if you allow it to. For that reason, I choose to stay away from watching or listening to the news as there's hardly ever anything positive or uplifting I can find there. The truth is that important news finds its way to me within hours anyway. I figure it is challenging enough to maintain a positive outlook on life most of the time, so why should I allow outside sources that are completely out of my control to affect my energy, thoughts and feelings that will create my actions and reality?

Do not get me wrong. I am not saying that positive thinking is all you need to manifest your dream life. However, I find maintaining positive thinking is quite helpful in maintaining that vibrational alignment to create what I desire rather than what I am trying to avoid.

Self-confidence and belief in your abilities play a huge role in proper manifesting. It is important to remember to keep your mind clear and shield itself from the outside influences of negative news, well-wishers, and naysayers who may be jealous or wish well but think they know better what is good for you.

3. **Patience and Trust.** Another key point I want to make is patience and trust. Having trust and being patient with yourself is trusting and being patient with the Universe, knowing that everything happens in divine timing, not in your limited way of thinking. The Universe is trying to create the best solution. The truth is that there are so many more solutions and options out there than you can imagine with your limited, two-dimensional way of thinking and seeing the world. It is also about the next key point coming up.

    To put it in context, had I not allowed the Universe to deliver my dream home to me in the divine timing (which, for me, took three years), combined with my own process of soul growth and self-understanding, I would have probably rushed into some decision of buying a wrong home or remaining in my old house. This means I could have possibly never found the happiness in the home I purchased by being patient and trusting that it existed and would be mine at the right time.

    Without connecting to your inner voice and having the self-confidence to stick to it, your ability to trust and patiently wait for the right time might waiver.

4. **Release Control.** Closely tied to trust and patience is knowing when and how to let go, specifically of control. It's about knowing what it means to surrender truly and that inner knowing and feeling of happiness of having your desire fulfilled before it's yours.

When trying to manifest something, you might anticipate having your desire fulfilled. Then, when you do not get it, or it doesn't come in the timeframe you establish, it is natural to get frustrated, upset, and sometimes angry. Instead of progressing, this takes you backward and away from the manifestation of that desire. I have certainly been a part of that numerous times in my experiences.

5. **Focus Forward.** To counter any arising agitation (when you do not release control), it is important to keep your focus forward. This is about keeping that energy, feeling, and emotion of excitement, happiness, and expectation of your realized desire rather than concentrating on the current immediate reality showing you that it's not here just yet. The moment your mind shifts to that negative mode of saying, "Oh, it is not here yet. When will I receive it? It's probably never going to happen," you are back to square one and vibrating at that lower frequency of lack.

6. **Preparation and Discipline.** The last way to train yourself to think differently is to understand that manifesting requires proper prep work and discipline. It's not likely that you can have nothing and then manifest extreme abundance overnight. There are steps required to instill some self-discipline to be ready to step into that abundance.

To me, it is a fun process. I treat it like a game, not as work of any kind. It is a game of life, and it is just a question of understanding its rules and then respecting and following them. Get set to create and manifest abundance!

From Lack to Plenty

Most people do not believe they have a scarcity mindset, but as I have shown through this chapter, your unconscious thoughts are inhibiting your ability to manifest. Here are some ways to shift things in your favor.

1. Shift your beliefs from scarcity to abundance. For example, instead of believing and saying you have to work hard to achieve anything in life, switch your dialogue to something like, "I can easily achieve anything I want."

    The Universe is showing you abundance in everything in nature. How many stars are in the sky? How many waves are in the ocean, sand particles on a beach, leaves on the trees, etc.? All the limitations come from your mind. Notice all the limitless opportunities that are everywhere if only you open your eyes and mind to see them and your heart to receive and accept them. Some people struggle with receiving, whether it's receiving gifts or compliments, and often you hold limitations around that. The opportunities are there, but how comfortable are you with receiving it?

    Similar is the idea that life is hard and then you die. You heard it somewhere and accepted it as truth. But the opposite can be just as true. Life is easy and fun!

2. Understand the cause vs. effect of what you are seeing in your life.

    Are you the driver or a passenger of life?

    What seeds are you planting in your mind and energy garden?

    What are you consuming?
    - **Mind:** *books, music, spoken words, knowledge*
    - **Body:** *food, exercise, rest, sleep*
    - **Spirit:** *positive energy, meditation, acts of kindness*

3. Take personal responsibility for your success. Then, decide to respond with gratitude or attitude.

4. Be aware of who you surround yourself with. Are they uplifting and encouraging you? Or are they bringing you down, keeping you playing small? There is a Native American fable representing the struggle that

goes on inside every human. It is a battle of two wolves—a dark and a light wolf. The dark wolf represents envy, arrogance, anxiety, ego, inferiority, regret, greed, self-pity, guilt, false pride, fear, pain, anger, jealousy, and rage; the light wolf represents love, peace, humility, kindness, serenity, generosity, trust, tranquility, compassion, empathy, joy, gratitude." The child asked, "Grandpa, so which wolf wins?" The grandfather responds, "Whichever one you choose to feed." Are the people you surround yourself with feeding the wolf of light or darkness within you?

5. Choose to step into abundance and receive it. It is already yours; you just need to step into it. Do you feel worthy of it? Is there a deep inner knowing that you deserve it? You are a precious being, deserving of the best, regardless of what anyone may say.

6. Approach your manifesting with wonder or curiosity to create certainty and help expand your energetic capacity for more. When you wonder about the specifics of an outcome, you have already assumed that the outcome will happen. You simply do not know the details and are curious about how everything will unfold. An example of this is if you are selling your house, you can think, I *wonder if the person who buys my house will be single or married.* Another idea is I *wonder where the extra $10,000 is going to come from.* You get the idea. Can you come up with a list of your own curiosities?

With the assistance of what you have learned in this chapter, you are ready to manifest and receive what you truly want. Remember, the manifestation mindset is that everything is happening *for* you, not *to* you. You do not know what you are capable of until you try it. As Neville Goddard said in *Awakened Imagination,* "The future must become the present in the imagination of the one who would wisely and consciously create circumstances. We must translate vision into Being, thinking *of* into thinking *from.*"

To become a butterfly, metamorphosis is necessary. If the caterpillar never went through this process of change, it would never achieve its great destiny and become its most glorious self. We can reach our great destinies by changing what needs to be changed.

Michelle 'Chaella' Boddie

Conclusion

By reaching this stage of my book, you have proven to yourself that you are already on the journey of metamorphosis from an unaware caterpillar with untapped potential to a butterfly with wings ready to unfurl gracefully, prepared to soar to new heights of self-realization.

In *Unhack Yourself*, you have been given a variety of tools designed to help you develop and improve your growth and wisdom; with time and practice, you will master them. From here on, give it time, put in the effort, and watch yourself become a pro at navigating life with these incredible resources at your fingertips. The STEER Method™ is designed to teach you how to master powerful strategies to navigate your experiences and allow a conscious knowing and connection to your inner voice, strength, and beauty. Dive into the exercises within this book and get ready to see your reality in a whole new light. Unhack Yourself is not just a book: it is your guide to flipping the script and transforming your entire life. I designed the STEER Method™ to teach you how to master powerful strategies to navigate your experiences and allow a conscious knowing and connection to your inner voice, strength, and beauty. With the exercises in this book and the STEER Method™, I hope you will have learned to perceive your reality in new ways and change your narrative, with newfound confidence to unhack yourself and transform your life.

To me, a journey towards transformation is about discovering your true self and being conscious and mindful of your thoughts, emotions, and (re) actions. By creating a positive emotional vibration, you can shift to align your inner world with your desired outer world. You have the power and the ability within you to change and rewrite your perspective of your life's stories, as the Universe is always listening, ready and waiting for you to live a limitless life. *Unhack Yourself* has broken down the steps to help you achieve desired outcomes.

Be open to letting your intuition guide
you rather than resisting it.

The first step to becoming a conscious author of your story is observing your thoughts, emotions, and (re) actions. Once you have this awareness, you need to consider how your perspective has created the stories and what you can do to shift your mindset to rewrite the narrative. Be open to letting your intuition guide you rather than resisting it. As you do this time and again, your intuitive muscle will grow stronger and create a shift in your energetic frequency.

How can you align your energetic frequency to your desired outcomes? This adjustment can include seeing, understanding and respecting the signs the Universe presents to you. By acknowledging these signs, you will attract more and more instances of positive experiences, leading to your life being more fun, joyous and harmonious. Know that the Universe is listening and is rigged in your favor.

However, it is possible you may have unconscious contracts that have previously shaped and defined your rules and beliefs and guided your actions and decisions. These stories can be the driving force for your limiting beliefs and behaviors. By discovering the origin of your unconscious contracts and understanding the potential benefits and consequences, you can use the STEER Method™ to rewrite your story and move forward towards the life you desire.

Emotions and beliefs affect everything you do and how you react. They can influence and significantly impact you physically and mentally. Sometimes, the effects of generational or emotional trauma can influence your life, resulting in adverse outcomes, including health, relationships, and financial issues. Rather than suppressing your emotions, let yourself experience emotions, but work on healing your emotional response. By learning to navigate your emotions, you get back into the driver's seat of your life as you restore your inner peace and learn to thrive even in the most turbulent times.

Sometimes, an unconscious block may limit your success in various areas, including finances, relationships, and how you see yourself. Once you identify those unconscious blocks, you can use that awareness and clarity to work on unblocking yourself by changing your perspective, thoughts, habits and words. It's time to focus on success and abundance by shifting your energetic alignment. Take the chance to unlock your unlimited potential with positive spoken and thought word choices, and use those affirmations to manifest what you desire. Remember, you have the power to make the necessary changes in your life.

Can you now imagine living a limitless life? How different could your life be, and what would you try next? The choices and possibilities are endless, and you are only constrained by your imagination. Part of retraining your mind to remove limits requires you to feel gratitude. Make sure your mindset is one of gratitude, including feeling grateful for what is possible, even if it has not yet occurred. By being grateful for future outcomes and not stressing about the outcome, the Universe is ready to make them happen. Harnessing the Law of Attraction, focus on the positive and reframe your thoughts around what you want rather than what you do not want. It is up to you to retrain your mind, be accountable for your thoughts, eliminate excuses, and take responsibility for your life. You can now choose how you perceive things and how you will react.

It is an entirely innate human characteristic to react to external circumstances, and it can sometimes mean the difference between life and death. However, being reactive and relying strictly on logic has consequences and can prevent you from being in the present. Instead, implementing a proactive approach and letting your intuition guide you can help you become more aware of your emotions and actions. You can let go of needing control, constantly chasing and achieving, and stop creating your karmic self-punishment. Flip your thinking to attract effortlessly. With various ways to shift your energetic vibration to match what you want, you can attract more positive experiences into your life. So, be proactive and try to live in the present moment.

It can seem daunting at first to live in a state of awareness as you work on eliminating limiting beliefs and negative programs and changing your thoughts to match and align with your goals, but gradually you begin to awaken and truly unhack yourself. The more you erase the outdated and unhelpful programs and beliefs you have unconsciously given power to and replace them with positive ones, the closer you get to the outcomes you desire. During this alignment process, there may be challenging times as your body, mind, and soul recalibrate and adjust to being upgraded. Embrace your awakening and the positive changes it brings.

By now, you understand the importance of thinking, believing, and receiving. Manifesting your desires and focusing on the "why" requires true alignment and becoming a vibrational match within your thoughts and beliefs, emotions and energetic state to consciously create your reality. You can achieve emotional liberation with acknowledgment and acceptance of painful emotions by allowing yourself to feel and process them fully. You are not a victim of your emotions; you are the one in control of your thoughts and feelings. Healing emotional trauma often requires forgiveness, either for yourself or others, and using tools like Ho'oponopono is one way to experience greater inner peace and emotional well-being. Suppressing emotions can lead to physical issues, so finding a way to release those negative emotions is essential.

Inner peace can only be created by those at peace with themselves. It cannot originate in an angry person. At times, we are empaths, and we feel others' stress and anguish. So, if you feel fear and anxiety come up for seemingly no apparent reason, try to tune in with your inner self and ask yourself, *Is this my own?* The answer may surprise you. You might realize that it's really not your own. Surely, there can be some physical reasons for it, such as a sugar imbalance or something else going on in your physical body, which can mimic the physical sensation of anxiety. For me, the healing journey of anxiety for many years was putting together the pieces of the puzzle and healing every part - mental, emotional, spiritual and physical harmony one step at a time.

The more you cultivate a sense of harmony within, the more you connect with your inner truth. In this transformative journey, it is crucial to allow

yourself to dream bigger, believe in yourself and remove doubts, fears and self-imposed limitations. This will help to align your subconscious programs with your conscious desires, paving the way to effortlessly manifest your dream life. Remember to set your intentions and be patient and confident, trusting the Universe to deliver on its own timeline, not yours. Your aspirations can become a reality. Imagine it and live it.

Throughout this journey of learning how to unhack your life, I have guided you on how to apply The STEER Method™ to achieve the results you desire. It is important to remember that your Results are directly related to the Story you tell yourself. The Thoughts that arise from those stories shift your Emotions and Energy accordingly, perpetuating the same negative loop. So, what story are you writing for yourself now? Is it helping your life move towards your goals, or are you repeating patterns that hurt and disempower you? If you are ready to make a change, then it's time to STEER your life towards success, abundance, and unlimited potential.

If you want to learn more about the STEER Method™, I invite you to visit:

https://www.healthandwealthcoach.com/steer-method

Know your true self and worth and that you possess an authentic consciousness within you that can make this happen. You are not broken; you can unhack yourself, complete a total system reboot, and restore to your natural default state. Be a caterpillar who trusts in their ability to soar like a butterfly. Embrace your journey of unhacking as you go through your metamorphosis to live an exceptional life.

I want to leave you with the Four Rs technique, which outlines my secret steps to success to help you continue to unhack parts of your life and achieve being the best you that you can be.

Step 1: **Reveal** the limiting beliefs and emotional blocks that keep you stuck.

Step 2: **Release** those beliefs and blocks.

Step 3: **Raise** your vibration and become aligned with your desired outcome.

Step 4: **Restore** your inner peace and sense of fulfillment.

If you are ready for a deeper transformation, I invite you to join me in an UnHack Yourself immersion experience, where you will be guided weekly to work through your blind spots, deep inner blocks, self-sabotaging thoughts and disempowering beliefs. You will learn to rewrite your life story and create a new, abundant life filled with happiness, success, and fulfillment.

As you conclude this transformative journey of Unhacking Yourself, I invite you to continue your growth and exploration in a more customized way. My coaching program is designed to provide personalized support, actionable strategies, and a community of like-minded individuals.

If you have resonated with the principles discussed in this book and are ready to take your next step, I would be honored to support you further.

Visit

https://www.healthandwealthcoach.com

to learn more and join a high-vibe community committed to making life-changing transformations.

Exercises to Unhack Your Life

———————— ◎ ————————

The following are example exercises taken from The STEER Method™ course.

Contraction vs. Expansion

While sitting, tighten your facial muscles and say, "I feel so happy." Did you feel happy? Probably not. It's hard to feel happy when contracted. Next, put your arms up and out, smile a big smile, and say, "I feel sad." Notice, do you feel sad? The goal is to practice living from an expanded space.

The Inner Ease™ Technique[17]

Put your hand on your heart and close your eyes. Breathe in love, ease, and compassion on every inhale. Next, ask yourself, "What is it my heart is calling me to do?" Ignore what the outside world tells you (not your friends, parents, or spouse). Pay attention to your heart and notice how it feels—become aligned with it. Do you notice what's happening to the world around you when you are feeling aligned? Now, feel the connection to everyone around you. Do you feel more expanded? Feel yourself sending that positive energy to the outside world. Emanate the love and kindness to the collective consciousness. Feel it, send it, and receive it. Share this love energy with the world around you. You can each help uplift yourself and others because we are all very interconnected. The butterfly effect. And do not forget: Your wisdom is in your heart, not your mind.

---

17 "Inner Peace through Inner Ease," HeartMath Institute, November 30, 2015, https://www.heartmath.org/articles-of-the-heart/heartmath-tools-techniques/inner-peace-inner-ease/

Exercise to Address a Particular Issue or Situation You're Dealing With

1. Describe the situation you'd like to address.

2. Notice what part of it is a story about it vs. the situation itself.

3. Describe the thought behind the story.

4. Observe the emotions this thought invoked and how it affected your entire energy, the way you feel, and the direction it caused you to go.

5. Rewrite that thought and choose a more empowering thought that will achieve your desired outcome.

Here are some helpful questions to use as a guideline to question your thoughts. Feel free to use your own questions.

Question Your Thoughts

When I think this thought, how does it make me feel?

What's the upside about me thinking this thought?

Is this thought one hundred percent true?

What behavior did this thought lead me to?

What result did I achieve by thinking, feeling, and acting that way?

Did it serve me well, or do I want to achieve a different outcome?

Can a different point of view (a different thought) about it be equally true?

What if I choose to believe a different thought? (Replace it with a more positive, uplifting, empowering thought.)

Notice how you feel now and use this method whenever you feel stuck.

How to Shift Gears from Fear into Faith

This process helps you shift your vibration immediately, and it works well, especially if you all of a sudden get overcome by negativity and fear, your mind starts spiraling out of control, and you need a quick way out and up. I recommend doing this daily.

1. I use a mantra as a reminder to shift my energy in that moment: "The Universe is rigged in my favor. Everything works out for the best."

2. Pay attention and notice your breath and your entire energy shift in that moment.

3. Shift from feeling constricted and holding tightness in your chest or stomach to feeling more expansive and allowing your breath to fully come through you. This creates an immediate shift in your vibration, which in turn affects your emotional state.

4. Keep that momentum.

5. If your mind wants to dwell on the negative and starts running the negative thoughts filled with "buts" and "what ifs," immediately and consciously reframe it to "What if something really good is going to come out of this? I'm just going to wait and allow the Universe to bring that good to me without trying to control the outcome."

6. Take a deep breath, hold it for a moment, and then breathe out.

Try to catch your thoughts, and the moment you feel them shifting somewhere negative, repeat this short exercise. In a matter of days, you'll be feeling a different vibration. As you do this more and more, you will start to experience positive things taking place in your life and less and less of the negative. You begin to align.

Always remember this: When you constrict (your energy), you restrict (the flow of abundance and love).

I believe that you are a spiritual being living a human experience, and a part of that experience is to also have situations come up that are unpleasant or difficult. However, it is quite empowering to know that you are the only one responsible for how you feel, and no one else can cause those feelings. This way, you are the one responsible for the steps you choose to take or not to take in your life and for the outcomes or the results you ultimately experience.

Here are some things to remember:

- *You are not your thoughts. You are the thinker of your thoughts.*
- *You can choose your thoughts and beliefs.*
- *You can question your thoughts and create different ones.*
- *Your thoughts affect the outcome you experience in your life, not the other way around.*
- *You can change your beliefs.*
- *You can allow yourself to experience all your feelings and let them process.*

Are you ready to seize control, unhack your mind, and begin your journey to steer the wheel of your life in the direction you are meant to go? Understand that your struggle does not stem from a lack of appropriate tactics or strategies. Nor is it because you lack persistence or willpower. Rather, it is rooted in the way you perceive and interpret the world around you. By shifting your mindset, you open yourself up to amazing new possibilities. The power to shape your reality lies within you; embrace it along with infinite possibilities that await.

Next Steps with Helen

You may be thinking now, "How do I get in touch with Helen Levine? I'm curious about working with her!" Below, you'll find her social media and website information. Feel free to connect on these platforms for updates and insights regarding Unhacking Yourself. Direct messaging options are also available.

Thank you for considering this opportunity. We look forward to the possibility of working together in the future.

www.instagram.com/healthandwealthcoach

www.linkedin.com/in/healthandwealthcoach

www.facebook.com/YourHealthandWealthCoach

www.healthandwealthcoach.com

About Helen Levine

Helen Levine is a renowned transformational coach, healer, and author recognized for her unique blend of personal insight, empathy, and wisdom. Helen's life journey inspires readers worldwide to reclaim their sense of self, embrace their inner truth, and create a fulfilling and purposeful life.

Through her writing and coaching programs, Helen empowers individuals to break free from limiting patterns and tap into their limitless potential. She is a master of manifestation who leads by example, having overcome her own struggles with burnout, scarcity, and toxic relationships.

Helen is happily married to her high school sweetheart, a loving mother of two incredible children, and a proud pet parent to a cherished 6lb Yorkie. Her mission is to create a ripple effect of healing and transformation by guiding individuals to heal themselves and their lineage, one person at a time.

Elevate Your Personal Growth with Unhack Yourself: The Workbook

Take the journey to become the best version of yourself with *Unhack Yourself: The Workbook* – the perfect companion to the transformative *Unhack Yourself* book.

This practical journal offers engaging exercises and ample space for notes, journaling, and reflection, helping you deepen your personal growth and self-discovery.

The workbook encourages you to engage actively with the concepts and techniques presented in *Unhack Yourself*. Each day, you can amplify your progress toward living your most fulfilling life.

Unhack Yourself: The Workbook serves as an essential addition to your self-help library, giving you the structure and support you need to apply the valuable insights from the book.

Find *Unhack Yourself: The Workbook* on Amazon and experience the incredible benefits of applying powerful strategies to your life. Embrace the journey to self-mastery and step towards a brighter, more fulfilling future.

www.ingramcontent.com/pod-product-compliance
Lightning Source LLC
Chambersburg PA
CBHW051309120626
46547CB00015B/2160